A LITTLE BIT

OF

DREAMS

A LITTLE BIT

OF

DREAMS

AN INTRODUCTION TO DREAM INTERPRETATION

STASE MICHAELS

STERLING ETHOS
New York

STERLING ETHOS
New York

An Imprint of Sterling Publishing
1166 Avenue of the Americas
New York, NY 10036

© 2015 by Stase Michaels

ISBN 978-1-4549-1301-6

Distributed in Canada by Sterling Publishing
c/o Canadian Manda Group, 664 Annette Street
Toronto, Ontario, Canada M6S 2C8
Distributed in the United Kingdom by GMC Distribution Services
Castle Place, 166 High Street, Lewes, East Sussex, England BN7 1XU
Distributed in Australia by Capricorn Link (Australia) Pty. Ltd.
P.O. Box 704, Windsor, NSW 2756, Australia

For information about custom editions, special sales, and premium
and corporate purchases, please contact Sterling Special Sales
at 800-805-5489 or specialsales@sterlingpublishing.com.

Manufactured in the United States of America

4 6 8 10 9 7 5 3

www.sterlingpublishing.com

CONTENTS

INTRODUCTION AND ACKNOWLEDGMENTS

First, a giant thanks to my family, who have always been my heart's first support team. And next, a heartfelt thank-you to the many dear friends who share my journey on the mystic path.

I dedicate this book both to those who are new to exploring their dreams and to those already on the daily dream adventure. Based on a lifetime of dream analysis, this book shares enough gems of insight to please one and all.

I cannot imagine living life without dream guidance, and thank all who came before me, who paved the way to self-understanding through dreams, starting with Carl Jung. Though I never met Jung, his seminal writing about dreaming continues to inspire. When I once asked a critical question about dreaming, he appeared as himself in a dream to answer my question. I felt greatly honored and cheered, as if he had passed the baton to me and to the many others who attempt to light the way. Many thanks to each of my former teachers at Atlantic University and to all who seek to explain the meaning of dreams.

Speaking of early influences, a great deal of my early understanding about dreams emerged by reading the twenty four published volumes of the Edgar Cayce readings that are available from the Association of Research and Enlightenment, in Virginia Beach. Cayce was a modern day mystic pioneer. He reportedly received his insights—while giving his psychic readings—by tapping into the "Akashic Records," a source of information theorized to be a compilation of the mystical understanding of life. The readings of Edgar Cayce are rich with references to dreams and their importance on the spiritual journey.

In my personal exploration of dreams, for years I kept condensing my dream analysis approach and it eventually evolved into the Five-Step Dream Technique described in this book. As a pivotal thought, I was first exposed to the idea of focusing on a "theme" or "story line" (step two of the Five-Step Dream Technique) by famed author Elsie Sechrist, who long ago wrote, *Dreams: Your Magic Mirror.* Elsie, who I had the privilege of knowing before she passed on, first alluded to generalizing the gist of a dream story at a seminar I attended. The thought has been refined and amalgamated into a quick and easy dream analysis method, proclaimed by newbies and those already on the journey as a great, fast-track tool.

Last but not least, I thank my terrific agent, Lisa Hagan of Paraview Books, a woman of great heart and brain power, and my editor, Kate Zimmermann, who wields a killer eye and pen in weeding out the content's riffraff. Kudos to their incredible work and support.

As the journey continues, it brings to mind some of my favorite lines of poetry. As Lord Alfred Tennyson wrote, "I am a part of all that I have met, yet all experience is an arc where thru' gleams that untraveled road whose margin fades, forever and forever when I move." May your trek of exploring your dream messages be as exciting as mine.

1

WHAT IS A DREAM?

HOW AUTHOR STASE MICHAELS ARRIVED AT A Definition of a Dream. When you have a dream, your first inclination is to wonder what it means. Few ask, "What is a dream?" and even as a dream expert, I did the same. For years, I focused on what the dream meant and never questioned what it *was*. From sleep lab studies, we know about Rapid Eye Movement (REM) sleep, brain wave activity during sleep, and sleep stages. However, such facts do not explain the origins or the function of a dream. Mystics, on the other hand, spoke of dreams as a message from the soul. That may be true, but again, does not define the mechanics of how a dream comes about. It finally dawned on me that I had no clear conception of what a dream really "is."

My curiosity led me on a ten year trek to find the answer. I read books and explored scientific journals. These helped me see what a dream *does*, but not what it *is*. The closest link to an answer emerged

1

from Freud's "day residue" idea which looks at dreams as leftovers about daily concerns, a concept later expanded by Montague Ullman. Dreams as day residue became the seed thought that led to a true definition. Mobilizing a lifetime of observations about dreams, a picture slowly unfolded about the mechanics of how a dream comes to be and what it *is*. As the pot of gold at the end of the rainbow, here is the ultimate definition of a dream, the one that satisfied.

WHERE DREAMS COME FROM

YOU JUGGLE TWO LIVES. You live two lives: an outer life of actions and an inner, hidden life of emotions and thoughts. These inner and outer parts of you are mediated by "the psyche," which, in the context of dreams, is defined here as your total interactions between your mind, your body, and for believers, your soul.

YOUR OUTER LIFE. As you go about your day, you carry out your roles as a parent, sibling, friend, student, doctor, bus driver, teacher, social worker, etc. Each role defines what you *do*, but does not define who or what you *are*.

YOUR INNER LIFE. While engulfed in daily routines, your mind conducts a silent, ongoing and internal dialogue as it matches up your immediate experience with what you think and feel. These inner-to-outer "matchups" may leave you feeling conflicted or feeling at peace. So many matchups get tacked on to your silent background bulletin board, that these memories of your daily experience pile up, and, like a stack of papers, they will eventually need to be sorted and filed.

THE PSYCHE AS A SILENT PARTNER. So much of your experience takes place during this silent, inner dialogue. Because this inner dialogue is a private conversation with yourself, ninety percent of what you think and feel remains unshared, even with your best friend or spouse.

THE PSYCHE KNOWS ALL, CONNECTS ALL. The part of you that does fully share in your inner conversation is the psyche. As your total inner self, the psyche blends your inner and outer lives and is the process that defines you as *you*. As your silent autopilot, the psyche is the "I" and "me" that is aware of all your thoughts, feelings, and actions. It acts as your main interface between yourself and the world, and acts as the best friend who has your interests at heart. The psyche represents the distilled thoughts and feelings that you arrive at, after sorting out all the inner chatter. Some call it the "inner voice." It is the traffic cop that filters what goes in and out of your brain and the administrator that later sorts and files your daily input of matchups between inner and outer lives.

The psyche is composed of:

- Mind, logic, and intellect.

- The awake, conscious part of you that steers your daily activity.

- The unconscious and unaware part of you that bubbles with hidden urges, concerns, thoughts, and feelings.

- The ideals, goals, and standards that comprise the "inner rules" by which you live your life.

- And when mobilized to do so, the psyche can connect you to your soul and act as a gateway to the divine.

COPING IN THE FAST LANE: LIFE MOVES TOO FAST. Whether you are caught up in work or play, most folks are constantly on the go and have little time to sort out what each day throws at them. With little time to think at the end of a long day, what happens to the overload of problems and concerns that you posted on your inner bulletin board?

THE BIRTH OF A DREAM

AN AUTOMATIC NIGHTLY REVIEW. Once you fall asleep, the mind turns on an "automatic housekeeping" button to filter and prioritize the day's events, feelings, and reactions. The mind now needs to handle the piled up inner-to-outer matchups from your day's experiences. The psyche kicks into gear and begins to review the leftover concerns, which Freud originally named "day residues." Esteemed dream pioneer, Dr. Montague Ullman highlighted such "day residues" as the seeds of a dream in his many books on dream interpretation. However, neither Freud nor Ullman explained how a dream actually unfolds. Stay tuned. Based on a lifetime of observation, this is how we see that a dream is born.

STEPS IN THE BIRTH OF A DREAM. The psyche's nightly review goes something like this:

A QUICK FIRST SCAN AND SORT. Like a high-speed computer, the psyche scans how the day's activities, thoughts, feelings, and observations, match up. It compares your *new* experiences to your similar *past* experiences. The psyche further observes how these new observations stack up against your goals, ideals, hopes, and wishes. During this first pass, the mind creates two piles: (1) the "completed" pile and (2) the "still needs attention" pile.

ITEMS IN THE "COMPLETED" PILE ARE FILED. The psyche first addresses the actions, thoughts, and feelings that were adequately handled and completed during the day. The items that have no emotional leftovers or loose ends are stored in memory. This is the equivalent of filing a stack of papers that no longer need your attention.

A SECOND, DELUXE SCAN TAKES PLACE FOR THE "STILL NEEDS ATTENTION" PILE. During the first scan, the "completed" pile was filed. During a second, more detailed scan, the psyche tackles the "still needs attention" list of unresolved thoughts, feelings, actions, and decisions that were triggered by the day's events. As if the mind were a high-speed computer, the psyche prioritizes your issues and flags the questions, unfulfilled desires, and problems that require your attention. It also compares unresolved issues against your current and past experience. The *end result* is a set of conclusions and suggestions about what could be done to resolve those issues, conclusions that the mind now needs to transmit back to you.

THE PSYCHE'S FEEDBACK IS CONVEYED AS A DREAM. After evaluating your ongoing concerns, the psyche cranks out a report to summarize whatever may have escaped your attention, as gleaned from the previous day's bulletin board notes. This report from the psyche may offer you a fresh perspective, a new insight, or a suggestion to get further information about a half-processed topic. As you sleep, this mini report is relayed to you in the form of a visual memo about your unresolved feelings, concerns, and decisions. You heard it here first—this mini report is otherwise known as a dream.

WHAT DOES A DREAM COMMUNICATE? A dream memo from the psyche can include one or more of the following topics:

- An overview of unresolved feelings or issues.

- Past influences or reactions that are relevant to a current issue.

- Current unnoticed factors that affect a topic.

- Feelings with which you may not be in touch.

- An invitation to change a perspective or a goal.

- Advice on how to deal with an issue.

- General or specific insights into a problem or concern.

PHYSIOLOGICAL EFFECTS ON THE BODY WHILE YOU DREAM

THE BRAIN STAYS ACTIVE. The brain is as active while you dream as it is when you are awake. The body may show physiological signs when you are in dreaming, such as rapid, irregular, or shallow breathing, an increase in heart rate, or a rise in blood pressure.

YOUR MUSCLES FREEZE. A little known fact is that when you dream, the large body muscles, like in your arms and legs, become immobile, as a temporary state of paralysis.

THE DREAMING AND WAKING STATES CAN OVERLAP. Though waking and dreaming are separate states of awareness, their boundaries are not always distinct and there can be a few rare moments of brief overlap. If you accidentally wake up at the end of a dream but are not yet quite awake—which can happen during an intense or scary dream—the effect can be startling. Your mind may still be partly lodged in the dream and yet partially awake. You may notice that you can't move, an experience people often cite with trepidation. Not being able to move during a dream is normal. The paralysis vanishes when the dream ends or as you fully awaken. This is simply an overlap experience between waking and dreaming.

YOU DO NOT SLEEPWALK WHILE HAVING A DREAM. A common misconception is that people sleepwalk because they are acting out a dream. Not so. Because your arms and legs *do not move* when dreaming, you cannot physically act out your dreams. People who sleepwalk are not actually dreaming, even though they may report vivid images. Sleepwalking is a type of sleep disorder that most often occurs during deep-sleep, which is stage three, the deepest phase of sleep.

THE BOUNCE-BACK EFFECT. If you lose or reduce your "dream time" for even one night due to a lack of sleep, the next time that you sleep, you will experience extra dreaming time, until you catch up. This bounce-back effect restores the missed dream time, an effect that highlights the importance of dreaming as a built-in, physiological mechanism.

DO DREAMS HAVE MEANING?

There is an ongoing debate about whether dreams are a vehicle for messages or whether dreams are random by-products of the brain.

Both sides of the argument are briefly summarized here.

THE ONGOING DEBATE. Though mystics have long seen dreams as a message from the soul, psychologists are not so sure. Researchers are divided. Some conclude that dreams have meaning, while others theorize that dreams are random images that have no intentional meaning or message. As the nature of scientific enquiry, the debate will continue.

DREAMS AS MEANINGLESS, RANDOM EVENTS. Those who see dreams as meaningless think that dream imagery is related to the random, spontaneous firing of brain cells (neurons), which fire like blinking lights that turn on and off. This process of brain cells turning themselves on and off is thought to be part of the brain's housekeeping and upkeep. Proponents such as Francis Crick and Graeme Mitchson suggest that cells in the hindbrain (the lower brain stem) spontaneously activate cells in higher brain centers (the cortex), which creates the nightly imagery that we call dreams. They see dreams as meaningless. In this view, the images you experience at night are random events that happen because individual brain cells fire at random (turn on and off) during the night.

DREAMS AS MEANINGFUL. Those who hold the view that dreams *do* have meaning agree with those who hold the opposite view—that brain cells engage in spontaneous firing. However, they consider that fact irrelevant. Instead of a focus on individual brain cells, they theorize that, like a computer, the brain has the equivalent of built-in software (neuronal mechanisms) that enables the mind to process thoughts, feelings, and experiences. One such software-like neuronal package relates to dreaming.

These psychologists point out that the brain has other similar processes conducive to information processing, such as the ability of children to learn complex language patterns. Linguist Noam Chomsky describes language patterns as "deep" versus "surface" structures; these are complex grammar and language patterns that children absorb without coaching, no matter what their language. In Chomsky's view, such an ability in children suggests that the brain has a built-in template related to language learning. Theorists who see dreams as having meaning, surmise there are similar brain templates associated with dreaming.

Researchers Aaron Greenberg and Milton Kramer concluded that dreams have meaning, pointing to studies that suggest dreaming is linked to maintaining emotional and psychological balance. Their studies on the dreams and sleep of traumatized war veterans and those with emotional disorders indicate dreams play a key role in regaining emotional stability. Their research revealed that story lines in dreams relate to actual events in a dreamer's life and to actual needs in a dreamer's life. In effect, Greenberg and Kramer independently concluded that dreams are meaningful.

DO DREAMS GIVE YOU A MESSAGE? Do dreams carry specific insights for dreamers? Apart from scientific debates and hypotheses, you can check out countless dream books and Web sites that describe the personal experiences of individuals who have experienced specific messages and meaning in their dreams. No matter what scientists may speculate or conclude, dream enthusiasts will continue to analyze their dreams.

~ 2 ~

HINTS ABOUT DREAMS AND DREAMING

DREAM HINTS AND INSIGHTS. LEARNING TO ANA-lyze dreams is a little bit like learning to drive a car. Applying the Five-Step Dream Technique (explained in later chapters) to analyze dreams is like learning to control a vehicle—how to turn on the engine, maneuver the wheel, the gas pedal, and the brakes. Once you get comfortable driving, you notice rules of the road and learn tips about oil changes, keeping tires balanced, and so on. What follows are a few rules of the road, including a list of tips about dream analysis. Some insights may even add a bit of zing to your daily trek—like watching for dreams about the future.

REASONS FOR ESP IN DREAMS

The possibility that dreams may contain ESP (Extra Sensory Perception) fascinates most people and brings up the question, "Can dreams really foretell the future?" Experience suggests they can. To some, that claim may sound like mysticism or mumbo-jumbo, and, for a lucky few, a dream about the future may indeed catapult them into a realm from "the beyond." However, there are also ways to examine glimpses about the future in dreams, in a logical fashion. Here are several ways that ESP in dreams may come about.

REASON 1: A NON-MYSTERIOUS EXPLANATION OF ESP IN DREAMS. In my experience, most dreams that relate to the future are "best guesses" about a question or a decision that is on your mind. Since the future is built on today's decisions, one way to think about ESP in dreams is that your dreams have the ability to reveal what path your current decisions are taking. For example, suppose you throw a ball down a hill. It is easy to guess whether the ball will hit a shrub, bounce on a boulder, or land in the stream. In the same way, your psyche, the part of your mind that is aware of all your decisions, lines up at the top of the hill and makes a best guess about where your decisions are heading. Such a best guess is accurate—*if and only if*—you remain on your current course.

REASON 2: FATE AND THE DIVINE HAND. A less common type of ESP dream emerges from the soul or from the divine hand. This form of ESP dream sends shivers up your spine because it defies logic as it predicts what is beyond. J. B. Rhine, a modern researcher of paranormal phenomena, logged a famous example. He described how, years ago, a handful of children in a Welsh mining village pre-dreamed that their school would collapse under an avalanche. Several days later, the event happened.

REASON 3: YOU PRE-DREAM EVERYTHING OF IMPORTANCE. In the same vein, Virginia Beach's famed mystic, Edgar Cayce, suggested that you pre-dream everything of importance that happens to you. Such dreams about the future that your soul portrays, may best be explained by what Shakespeare's Hamlet said to Horatio: "There are more things in heaven and earth, Horatio, than are dreamt of in your philosophy." Some things are yet beyond our ken.

FUN DREAM FACTS AND HINTS

Like adding a G.P.S. system to a car, these facts and tips can steer you in the right direction to maximize your dream analysis benefits.

Hint 1: Dreams Communicate in Images Because of How the Brain Works

A dream speaks in pictures because your brain is hardwired to remember visually. As psychologists have confirmed, the brain stores much of its information (i.e., thoughts, memories, and experiences) as images that are linked up to your thoughts and feelings—becoming a mental picture in the mind's eye. This is why visual pictures are the language of the brain. That is also why, in books on how to boost your memory, you are asked to link the words or names that you want to remember with a set of images, in order to remember them. When it comes to memory and your brain, pictures rule!

Hint 2: All Dreams Are Meaningful.

All dreams carry a message, and even a single dream image has meaning. Some dream messages are about your emotions while others relate more to your thoughts, attitudes, or actions. For example, in one such single-image dream, a man saw a large wooden wheel. At first, the image seemed meaningless, but later he remembered that when he was growing up, there had been a wagon wheel on his family's farm. After his mother died, he often sat beside that wagon wheel as he mourned. The dream image of the wheel made him realize that he still felt bad about the recent loss of a good friend. The dream suggested he needed to take the time to grieve for his friend, just as he had grieved by the wheel for his mother.

Hint 3: Everyone Does Dream.

Those who say they do not remember any dreams often wonder if they dream at all. Research confirms that everyone experiences dreams. In fact, you dream about four to six times a night, whether or not you remember any of your dreams. Dreaming and recalling your dreams are two separate issues.

Hint 4: There Are Several Sources of Dream Messages

SOURCE 1 OF DREAM MESSAGES: YOUR MIND. Most dreams are communications from your psyche, the inner part of you that is aware of all your experiences, goals, and memories. Like a best friend, the psyche (your inner self) acts like a bridge between your waking and sleeping self and uses dreams to guide you to be the best you can be.

SOURCE 2 OF DREAM MESSAGES: THE SOUL AND BEYOND. Some dream insights come from the soul. You may be the captain of your ship but the soul is the ship's owner, and on occasion, the soul has something to say about your path in life. Speaking of the great beyond, many believe that guardian angels can whisper in your ear through a dream, and that, on occasion, the divine itself bestows experiences of amazing grace, healing, or inspiration in dreams. Many dreamers have confirmed such extraordinary dream events.

SOURCE 3 OF DREAM MESSAGES: THE DEARLY DEPARTED. Some individuals believe that life continues after death and that dreams reconnect you with a loved one who has passed on. Anecdotal dream experiences suggest that the dearly departed visit on occasion to let you know they still love you (see Chapter 11, "Not All Dreams Are Dreams").

Hint 5: Dream Analysis Is Easy.

There is a general misconception that learning to understand the message in a dream is difficult; however, if you can learn to drive a car, you can learn to analyze your dreams. Dream analysis is about understanding the language of symbols and metaphors and orienting yourself to a few rules of the road, such as the hints listed below. Once you master these concepts, you will be on your way.

EASY ANALYSIS HINT 1: LEARN THE BASICS. Become familiar with the basics of dream interpretation such as those described in the Five-Step Dream Technique, which is introduced in later chapters. Once you crack open the nut of meaning of a dozen dreams, you will be on your way to a lifetime of amazing dream messages.

EASY ANALYSIS HINT 2: LOOK FOR THE "AHA" EFFECT. When the meaning of a dream comes together, you get an "Aha!" rush of energy as a notable shift in perception. Understanding a dream message brings satisfaction, like watching a final puzzle piece fit into the big picture.

EASY ANALYSIS HINT 3: BEWARE OF PERSONAL BIAS. Everyone has topics that trigger emotional reactions and sweep them away. Because of this, approaching a dream without preconceptions or reactions is important. If the topic of a dream is too intense, take a step back to avoid slanting your potential interpretation toward wishful thinking. Since initial reactions can steer you off course, a cool head is key to a correct interpretation. To correctly analyze a dream, put aside tinted eyeglasses and be willing to accept the truth, the whole truth, about the dream's meaning.

EASY ANALYSIS HINT 4: PUT AN INITIAL GUESS ON HOLD. As you wake up with a dream, the excitement of the story makes it easy to decide that you already know what it means. Hold that confidence in check and decide that you *do not* know what the dream means, at least not yet. As you apply the dream analysis techniques of your choice, your perspectives may shift and may bring a different result than your first thoughts about the dream.

EASY ANALYSIS HINT 5: NOTE YOUR WORD CHOICES. Notice which words you select as you record your dream. The words that come to mind often alter your thoughts about the dream itself and create a shift in perception. This word-choice phenomenon is another way that the creative, unconscious mind reveals glimpses into the meaning of a dream.

EASY ANALYSIS HINT 6: SYMBOLS ARE NOT THE WHOLE DEAL. A common misstep is to focus *only* on the meaning of a symbol and attempt to find dream message from the symbols, or to focus on the symbols first. Though dream symbols add depth to the message, focusing mainly on symbols tends to be a misstep. There are dreams where a symbol holds the entire message, but in general, the overall story tends to be the key to understanding the dream.

EASY ANALYSIS HINT 7: YOU CAN DO IT. Despite these caveats, proceed without fear. Dream analysis is as easy as learning to drive a car. Once you know how to start the engine and observe a few rules of the road, you are on your way to dream analysis.

EASY ANALYSIS HINT 8: DREAMS AS A LUXURY VEHICLE TO GET THROUGH LIFE. Having paid attention to dream messages all my life, to me it appears as if those who do not analyze their dreams are trying to get through life using a bicycle. They miss out on a fantastic built-in Rolls-Royce of the mind—dream insights—that can get them where they want to go faster, more securely, and at their own speed.

Hint 6: Frightening Dreams Are Constructive Messages.

Even though a scary dream shakes you up, most nightmares carry a helpful message. The most common type of nightmare invites you to repair a character trait in yourself. Here's how that works. In general, since people do not care to face something unpleasant about themselves, they push away a dream that makes them feel as if they are being scolded. As the dreamer pushes such a dream away—which, in psychological terms, is an attempt to suppress the dream—the dreamer's clouded awareness "masks" the dream's content. As a result, like seeing something in the distant, murky shadows, a friendly image now appears scary. Watching a dream about a personal flaw can feel like meeting an enemy in a deep, dark, empty forest. It is an "oops" that frightens the fragile ego, which reacts with "Who, me?" Though a rare nightmare can be a literal ESP dream warning, most scary dreams are distorted, but helpful, messages about your own flaws.

Hint 7: Dreams Help You Solve Problems.

As one of the main functions of dreaming, dreams can help you make decisions, clarify questions, and resolve daily challenges. In fact, experience dictates that the default stance of the sleeping mind is to assist you with any knot that you are trying to untie. Like a night-time Google session, your mind investigates the topic of your concern, compares the issue to your storehouse of past and current experience, and then cranks out an insight or a solution. Taking the time to plug into this "default nightly brainstorming" session can be highly productive on a wide range of matters, from advice to the lovelorn, daily questions, or even to achieve a scientific breakthrough.

Hint 8: Dream Messages Are Metaphors.

Dreams often exaggerate to make a point and most dream scenes are rarely literal. They are metaphors, and it helps to keep that in mind. For example, a scene about an avalanche that is going to engulf your home may scare you, but unless you live on a susceptible mountainside, the image is a metaphor about something that threatens your security, is off track, or is out of control. Positive scenes are also metaphors. A dream of winning the lottery suggests that you are a big winner, but what you are winning is not likely money. The win can signal career advancement, a great new relationship, or a talent that is being acknowledged—as your own kind of winning ticket.

Hint 9: Dream Dictionaries Cannot Tell You What a Dream Means

At best, a good dream dictionary can give you a general idea about what a symbol may mean, but it cannot tell you what that symbol actually means in the context of your specific dream. Dream dictionaries are a cookie-cutter approach to images. In contrast, the best part of a dream symbol is that it is a one-of-a kind communication uniquely tailored to you and in most cases, does not apply to anyone else. Check out the chapter on Symbols to get the exact and true meaning of dream images.

Hint 10: You Are the Best Interpreter of Your Dreams.

Once you learn the basics and stack up a dollop of experience, you become the best interpreter of your dreams. The reason is that dreams are about you and your life. Since you are the most familiar with the life areas about which your dreams speak, you are the best interpreter of your dreams.

Hint 11: What to do with a Cryptic Dream.

For every effort that you make to understand a puzzling dream which leads to a successful insight, it becomes easier to interpret the next dream. However, when you *do* come across a puzzling dream, there are a few options.

1. Wait awhile and try again a few hours later or a few days later.

2. Talk it over with a friend; sometimes the comments of a sympathetic listener can add new perspectives.

3. Browse through the example dreams at InterpretADream .com, check out books on dreams, or poll the Internet on specific dream topics.

THE BENEFITS OF A DREAM JOURNAL

If you jot down a dream as soon as you wake up, recording your dreams will become routine. Whether you record dreams on a computer or in a notebook, there are benefits to having a permanent record of your dreams.

Dream Journal Hint 1: Why Keeping a Dream Record Helps You Get the Message

BENEFIT 1: YOU LOCK IN A DREAM MESSAGE. By recording a dream, you lock in its message. Otherwise, the odds are that you will forget the dream and lose whatever insight it is trying to share. If time is short, jot down key phrases and record the full version later.

BENEFIT 2: IT KEEPS YOU IN TOUCH WITH YOUR PSYCHE. Recording a dream ensures that messages will keep coming. Dream communications are like talking to a friend, which, in this case, is your psyche or inner voice. If you do not return a friend's calls or e-mails, they stop. Recording your dreams tells your psyche that you want to keep talking and hearing the advice your inner voice has to offer.

BENEFIT 3: YOU SEE CRITICAL PATTERNS. A dream journal lets you notice patterns that relate to your emotional battles, decisions, relationships, and finding your path in life.

BENEFIT 4: YOU NOTICE WARNINGS OR A POSITIVE HEADS-UP. It is said that you pre-dream everything of importance that happens to you. Whether a dream brings a health warning or is a heads-up about a promotion, recording your dreams regularly is like maintaining a flashlight on life's dark roads. It can shed light on the unknown.

BENEFIT 5: IT IS EASIER TO TRACK YOUR PSYCHOLOGICAL PROGRESS. Dreams unveil patterns about your psychological and emotional health. Each time you spot a pattern in your dream journal, you empower your own progress. Plugging into those patterns via dreams can make a striking difference to the success, peace, and happiness that you achieve.

BENEFIT 6: A DREAM JOURNAL CAN BE A SPIRITUAL DIARY. If spirituality is important to you, your dream journal becomes a reflection of your inner life. For those who keep an eye on their spiritual progress, dreams can connect you to your soul. Many traditions value dreams as a spiritual connection and perceive dreams as a door to divine healing and blessings. Spiritual dreams are messages that relate to the journey of your soul and can answer life's big questions. A dreamer who had never felt that God was real asked herself, "God, are you there?" She received a dream that knocked her socks off and the experience left her convinced that God personally knew her and loved her unconditionally. She described the dream experience as feeling more loved than she had ever felt in her life. Whatever your spiritual questions, staying active with a dream journal helps such experiences unfold.

BENEFIT 7: A DREAM JOURNAL CAN BE THERAPEUTIC. Need a therapist? One key function of dreams and dreaming is to serve as a built-in counselor. The very act of dreaming may in and of itself help to relieve stress and keep your emotions in balance. At the same time, dreams often unearth insights with the deft hand of a loving counselor. At other times, jarring images may arise to get your attention when you are emotionally veering off track. Don't laugh. Maintaining an active dream journal can feel like instant therapy.

Dream Journal Hint 2:
It Pays to Review Your Dream Journal

REASON 1: A REVIEW IS A FAST TRACK TO NOTICE INSIGHTS AND SOLUTIONS. Every time you sift through past dream messages, your dreams become clearer. It's like getting to know a new friend. Over time, you understand each other better and can help each other more. After you review your dreams, your psyche may begin to fast-track new, amazing insights and solutions. Reviewing such insights that were logged in a dream journal can be especially valuable for those in professions that require problem solving.

REASON 2: GOING THROUGH YOUR DREAMS HELPS YOU GAIN A FRESH PERSPECTIVE. Whether it is months or years later, reviewing your dreams can be the equivalent of taking an inventory of your life, who you are, and where you are at. You may notice emotional patterns to which you were previously blind and may decipher dreams whose meaning had escaped you. As you explore with fresh eyes, you see deeper meaning in certain dreams and discover further revelations about yourself and your life. As you take a trek through your dream journals, magical ongoing threads that recount the story of your life can unfold.

Dream Journal Hint 3:
What to Put into a Dream Journal

Tricks for Dream Entries. Recording a dream may seem obvious, but there are a few tricks that are worth noting. Recording a dream is *not* the goal—the goal is to understand the dream's message and to apply it. Including the following items as you record your nightly tales can improve your dream skills.

DATE. Note the date; someday, when you look back, it will be of interest.

TITLE. Give each dream a separate title that highlights its main impact.

DETAILS. Record every detail, even if you think it is unimportant or repetitive; such details may later prove important.

AS IF IT IS HAPPENING. Write the dream in the present tense, as if you are re-experiencing it. Doing so often helps recall extra details or fill in a scene you had previously forgotten.

FEELINGS. Note how a dream made you feel. The mood that a dream brings out in you can be a clue to its meaning.

A ONE-LINE SUMMARY. Immediately jot down a quick story line, as if writing a movie trailer that explains what your mini movie dream is about. Let this one-liner capture the heart of the dream, as your first impression about the dream.

LIFE CONTEXT. Make brief notes about your life. The question to ask yourself is always, "To what in me or to what in my life does the dream refer?" It may take a week or two to get an "aha" for every dream, and if you lose the thread of what was happening at the time, you are less likely to zero in on the message. Jot down brief reminders about:

- What was on your mind as you went to sleep.

- Major feelings you have been experiencing.

- Main issues that day, that week, or that period.

- Major pending decisions.

- Challenges, crises or turmoil related to relationships or other circumstances.

DREAM RECALL HINTS:
WAYS TO REMEMBER YOUR DREAMS.

Whether you have trouble recalling dreams in general, or want to remember more, try these tips.

RECALL HINT 1: GET ENOUGH SLEEP. If tired, you are less likely to remember a dream. If necessary, catching up on sleep over the weekend can be a great way to improve dream recall.

RECALL HINT 2: GIVE YOURSELF A PRESLEEP SUGGESTION. If you are new to dreams or having trouble with recall, before falling asleep, tell yourself in a relaxed manner that you will remember your dreams. Giving yourself a presleep suggestion informs your psyche that you are ready and willing to communicate. However, if doing so feels intense or scary, you may not be ready to investigate your dreams, even if their messages are positive and helpful. There is no rush; wait until the thought of understanding your dreams feels comfortable.

RECALL HINT 3: MAKE IT EASY. Keep paper and pen handy. If you don't have time to record the full dream, jot down the gist and add the specifics later.

RECALL HINT 4: RECORD SOMETHING. If you do not recall a dream when first starting out on your dream journey, note the feelings, ideas, or new thoughts that hover as you wake up. These may be remnants of a dream message and recording them can help with future dream recall.

RECALL HINT 5: MOTIVATION. Be eager to remember your dreams.

Your psyche needs to get the message that you are ready and willing to hear its messages, and enthusiasm will start the ball rolling.

RECALL HINT 6: STAY RELAXED AND FIND SOME DOWN TIME. If you have not worked with your dreams before, taking a few minutes of quiet time for yourself each day can help forge a path to your psyche. Anything that allows you to unplug from intense daily activities will work. A short meditation, music, a walk in nature, or a creative hobby can help synchronize your outer and inner parts.

RECALL HINT 7: APPLY WHAT YOU GET. Once you have a dream and zero in on its meaning, apply the message. Like taking advice from a good friend, dream advice will keep coming if you listen to it.

WHAT CAN INTERFERE WITH DREAM RECALL. SEVERAL FACTORS MAY CONTRIBUTE TO NOT BEING ABLE TO REMEMBER YOUR DREAMS, AS LISTED HERE.

BLOCKAGE 1 TO DREAM RECALL: A LACK OF INTEREST. The most common reason people do not remember their dreams is a lack of interest. If you become enthusiastic about what your dreams have to say, recall tends to improve dramatically.

BLOCKAGE 2 TO DREAM RECALL: MEDICATIONS AND ALTERED STATES. Alcohol, some prescription medications, and street drugs can interfere with dream recall. This may include some sleep meds, whether they are the over-the-counter kind or were prescribed for short-term use.

BLOCKAGE 3 TO DREAM RECALL: DEEP PAIN. When coping with

intense personal loss or pain, a person sometimes shuts down emotionally. This can, at times, result in a loss of dream recall. Once the pain is dealt with, the person may again remember their dreams.

BLOCKAGE 4 TO DREAM RECALL: POST-TRAUMATIC STRESS. Trauma such as war experiences or natural disasters that lead to loss and destruction can create a medical condition known as post-traumatic stress. For some, trauma produces long-term nightmares and can shut down their recall, other than the nightmares that replay the catastrophe. Traumatic nightmares are more intense and show physiological and psychological differences to regular nightmares. As the trauma is resolved, normal dreams and natural sleep patterns may be restored, including remembering one's dreams.

THE FIVE STEP DREAM ANALYSIS TECHNIQUE: A FAST TRACK TO THE MEANING OF YOUR DREAMS.

You Need Only Five Minutes to Analyze a Dream

This is a first glance at a quick method to analyze your dreams in five easy steps, as summarized below. Further details about each step follow in Chapters 3 through 7.

Discovering what your dreams mean is as easy as learning to ride a bicycle. Use these five steps to get your balance on a dozen dreams and you will be on your way to a lifetime of dream insights. Once you get into the rhythm, you can begin to see the meaning of many dreams in five minutes.

Step 1: Emotions.

Note your feelings (1) during the dream and (2) as you wake up. Your emotional reaction to a dream is the first clue to what it means, and on occasion, your reaction is the most important clue. For example, if you see yourself lying in a coffin but you wake up feeling happy, the dream is not likely a prediction of your demise.

Step 2: Story Line.

The story line is a generalized "restating" of the dream *without* repeating the actual details. It is *not* a summary. A summary merely extracts the main ideas using the same terms as the original story. To get the story line, you extract the main action and the end result of the dream *without* using the *actual* words. You replace the story's original words with general terms like "someone" or "something."

Clear as mud so far? The following examples will clarify what a story line sounds like. This step may take a smidgeon of practice, but since it is often a key turning point to finding the meaning of a dream, it is well worth the effort.

FOR EXAMPLE, a young man dreams that he is trying to catch a firefly on a warm summer night. He swats at the fireflies yet keeps missing; he chases one, but it gets away. Out of frustration he plunks down on the grass and sits quietly. As he relaxes, a firefly gets close and he gently catches it.

THE STORY LINE IS: "Frantic activity fails, but someone succeeds after becoming quiet." Or "Someone gets what they want by staying calm and letting it come to them." Each version of the story captures the gist of the dream, but there is no direct mention of the young man, a firefly, or sitting on the grass. Like a silhouette, the story line ignores the details and, instead focuses on the story generalizations and results. By doing so, what is important comes into focus.

Step 3: Match the Story Line to an Area of Your Life.

As always, the question is not "What does this dream mean?" The question is, "To what in my life (my actions, decisions, or relationships) or in me (my personality, attitudes, or emotions)—does the dream refer?" Like fitting a puzzle piece into the big picture of your life, determine what, in you, or in your life, may sound like the story line. Examine the story line gist you just put together as if it is an arrow pointing to a situation, a trait, or an attitude.

You can turn the story line into a question. That can help you see where the arrow points. For example, in the above dream about the young man and the firefly, the dreamer might ask himself, "Am I frantic in some area of my life?" Or "What issue could be resolved if I stay quiet instead of pushing?" Once the story line matches an area of your life, the message often clicks.

Step 4: Symbols.

The brain is hardwired to visually record and remember your memories, thoughts, and events. As a result, most memories are "pictures linked to feelings," which is important to note. Since the brain stores memories as images, it is no surprise that dreams—which are a by-product of the mind—also use pictures to communicate their message.

Dream symbols are pictures that relate to and are "linked to" memories and experiences such as graduating from school, receiving flowers, or a special exchange with a loved one. Because a dream symbol has an emotional link to your past, a symbol leaves an emotional footprint on your heart and can speak volumes. That is why—when you explore a dream symbol such as a flower or a piece of jewelery—you examine it in two ways. First, see how the image makes you feel, and second, check out what past experiences the symbol relates to, in your life. This two-pronged approach to dream symbols—the feelings a symbol evokes and the memory it relates to—is called "exploring your associations." You examine the related emotions and you examine where, when, and how that particular image or scene touched your life. Like Hansel and Gretel leaving a trail of crumbs through the woods, that trail of your associations will lead you to what the dream symbol means.

For example, you see a red sports car in a dream and it makes you feel elated. Later, you remember that when you graduated from college, you fantasized about reaching the top of the corporate ladder and driving a sports car. In this case, the feelings and past memory of the red sports car relates to those early motives to achieve in career, and as a message, the symbol invites you to assess how far you have come to reaching your goals.

Step 5: What the Dream Means.

By the time you run a dream through steps one to four, you have noticed your feelings (step one), created a story line and matched it to a real-life situation (steps two and three), and observed how its main symbols relate to your personal experience (step four). By that time or anywhere along the way, an "aha" moment often comes together to reveal the dream message.

Discovering what the dream is telling you is half of the game; the other half is to apply the insight. A dream is practical and useful—*if and only if*—you apply its insight. Step five is about applying what you get from the dream into your life. Whether the message invites you to change an attitude, explore career options, or expresses congratulations for a job well done, using a dream message is like building a solid house, one brick at a time. Every time you apply a new insight to your life, it is like adding a brick to a mansion you are creating. Its application helps you unleash your potential one step at a time and puts the odds in your favor of achieving success, peace, and happiness.

~ 3 ~

EMOTIONS
AS
DREAM FLAGS

EMOTIONS AS THE MUSIC OF YOUR DREAMS. NOT everyone is a music aficionado, but you know when a song or a piece of music pleases you. Great music can alter your feelings, bring longing into your heart, or incise a wound you forgot was there. By the same token, listening to music that you do not care for is like hearing a discordant clash of sounds; it can make you cringe or back away. Emotions are the music of your dreams. Whether a dreams uplifts you or makes you balk, your reaction is part of the message. Not only are the emotions *within* the dream important; the emotions you feel *as you wake up*, are also meaningful. Did you go to sleep feeling unhappy, then woke up floating on a cloud and feeling great, after a dream? Did a dream jolt you awake, filling you with trepidation? It is all part of the emotional music in dreams, as explained here.

STEP 1: EXAMINING EMOTIONS IS STEP ONE OF THE FIVE-STEP DREAM TECHNIQUE

EMOTIONS AND DREAM MESSAGES. According to step one of the five-step technique, what you feel *during* the dream or what you feel *about* the dream after you wake up are the first clues to its meaning. If you see a huge lion enter your yard, yet it lies down, looks friendly, and you feel content at the sight instead of terrified, the positive feelings indicate that the message is not about being in danger. Or suppose you dream of your spouse in the kitchen losing their temper and smashing a plate in anger, but in the dream you remain calm and continue to wash the dishes. The dream may speak of the angry sparks that flew during an actual disagreement between you and your spouse, yet your serene attitude in the dream hints that the real-life situation can be resolved by staying calm.

STRONG DREAM EMOTIONS GET YOUR ATTENTION. A dream scene can pack an emotional punch and it does so to get a point across about an issue that needs your attention. A scene of almost drowning can be a metaphor for feeling overwhelmed, a child having a tantrum may indicate someone acting childish or a circumstance veering out of control, and an explosion may relate to an explosive relationship or situation. When a dream creates supercharged metaphors that affect your emotions, the strong reaction you feel to the images is a red flag that tells you the message is important.

YOUR REACTION TO A DREAM CAN JUMPSTART CHANGE. Suppose you have a dream that creates feelings of emotional upheaval in you for hours or even days. Though that sounds bad, sometimes a dream deliberately "creates" turmoil in you to stimulate a change in you. Intense reactions that leave you reeling, emotionally, can invite a change in attitude or push you into a new perspective. For example, a senior in college who is slacking off from his studies dreams that he has failed a final exam and will not graduate. The dream feels so real that it scares him into studying. Or, a man in a dead-end job dreams that everyone around him gets promoted, except him. The anguish the dream evokes in him spurs him to investigate ways to move forward in his career.

EXAMPLE 1 OF DREAMS THAT JUMPSTART YOUR FEELINGS: HAVING SEX WITH SOMEONE YOU DESPISE. Dreams of having sex with someone you cannot stand are common. A woman dreams that she has sex with a boss she despises, yet to her surprise, the passion in the dream feels real and magnificent. She wakes up confused, aware that she hates her boss but finding it hard to dislike someone with whom she has just had great sex. Because of the dream, her feelings of hate for him are now in flux; the dream softens and changes her attitude to her boss, allowing her to make a fresh start in the relationship.

When people dream about having sex with someone they dislike, their first thought is that the dream points to a secret attraction to that person. Usually, that is not the case. Instead, because prolonged animosity toward another is unhealthy (emotionally and psychologically), the psyche manufactures an intense, pleasant experience to jumpstart a change in attitude about that person. A wise man once stated that the best way to deal with an enemy is to turn him into a friend. A dream of having sex with someone you hate arrives as a peacemaker, initiated by your psyche.

EXAMPLE 2 OF DREAMS THAT JUMPSTART YOUR FEELINGS: BLESS-INGS FROM A DECEASED LOVED ONE. A depressed man dreams of his dead father, the only person who truly understood him. The father hugs his son, tells him how proud he is of him, smiles, and then disappears. The dreamer wakes up elated; his depression has lifted.

Dreams that jumpstart a change can at times accomplish more than hours of encouragement by a friend or therapist, and can have an ongoing impact on the dreamer.

DREAMS AS A THERMOMETER OF YOUR FEELINGS. In life's daily rush, it is easy to get out of touch with your emotions. When riding a roller-coaster of ups and downs, dreams can help you notice your feelings and cope with the problems behind those jangled emotions.

At times you may ignore your feelings or feel overwhelmed by them. Dreams help you notice your feelings and label them, so that you can begin to deal with them. Watching yourself in a dream where you are riding a merry-go-round that will not stop can feel terrifying, and can be a metaphor for feeling emotionally out of control. Or, seeing yourself parachute out of an airplane, gliding joyfully through the sky, may put you in touch with the pride you feel about a successful accomplishment.

Suppose you are trying to be patient with an annoying work associate but they still drive you crazy. One night you dream that you punched out the co-worker. The dream is *not* suggesting that you hit your associate. Instead, the dream mirrors your frustration and invites you to fix your reactions to that associate, reactions that are creating knots in your feelings.

A dream can also indicate whether your emotions are surging or sinking. If a shy man dreams of giving orders at work as if he were a drill sergeant, the dream may hint that he needs to speak up and is capable of doing so; it invites him to come out of his shell. If a confident businesswoman dreams that her staff hide under their desks when she walks by, the dream is hinting that her confidence has veered into overbearing. It invites her to soften her stance with her employees.

EMOTIONS AS A MESSAGE TO SELF. Counselors often view emotions as "messages to yourself." For example, a scene of depression in a dream can point to a hidden hurt that needs to be expressed. Anger can point to strong feelings that need to be channeled into leadership. Arrogance may mask a lack of confidence or indicate a desire to be appreciated. When the emotional impact is strong or leaves you puzzled, see whether the emotions are a message to yourself.

4

THE STORY TELLS ALL: HOW A STORY LINE EMBODIES THE DREAM MESSAGE

I T'S THE STORY, STUPID. WHEN MOST PEOPLE THINK of analyzing a dream, they immediately look at a symbol that captures their attention and dive into what that symbol means. Or, they focus on what a dream character may represent, as if a symbol or person in the dream holds the message. My mission as a dream expert is to shift the focus to the *dream story*. Shifting the emphasis from dream symbols does not imply that a symbol is not important—it is. However, in most dreams, symbols play a supporting role in the story. Why? Because a dream is a story about your life, and like a fairy tale that embeds a moral in its tale, the dream story *itself* holds the message. For example, suppose the fairy tale about Little Red Riding Hood, was a dream. It is a story about a naïve person who is almost fooled by a wolf in sheep's clothing; in this case, the dream would be a message about not being fooled by someone. That could be a con man selling bad stocks, or a cheating husband who speaks of leaving his wife to seduce a pretty girl. Whether the dream characters are portrayed as a smiling con man, a wolf in sheep's clothing, or a charming lothario, the message would be the same—watch out for someone's conniving schemes. Though there are always exceptions, in most dreams the story carries the main message. As this section explains in detail, understanding the "story line" of a dream is goal number one—and the foremost strategy—to discovering the dream's message.

STEP 2: CREATING A STORY LINE IS STEP TWO OF THE FIVE-STEP DREAM TECHNIQUE

Redefining the Story Is Key to Finding the Dream Message

Defining the gist of a dream is step two of the five-step technique. As you recall, the story line is a one-line statement that, if put together well, cracks open the meaning of the dream. Redefining the story into a story line is the fastest and most accurate path to the meaning of a dream. As the following examples show, it can be the critical turning point to finding the message and works for most dreams.

THE MAIN POINT TO CREATING A STORYLINE IS TO GENERALIZE.

To find the story line, make a broad statement about the actions and outcomes in the dream, without citing the story details. Extract the essence of the dream and restate it using words like "someone" and "something" to generalize what is happening. Creating such a generalization gets you past the obvious and eliminates distracting details.

EXAMPLE 1 OF FINDING THE STORY LINE: A STRANGER COMES CLOSE.

A young married woman in South Africa dreamed that she was a passenger in a car that was being driven by a handsome stranger. The driver leans across her lap to change gears and also to close a broken door on the passenger side. Closing that door creates a "walled-in" space. She feels a lot of physical attraction to him and they kiss. In the dream, this experience makes her very happy. But when she wakes up, as a woman who loves her husband and would never cheat on him, the dream leaves her feeling upset and confused.

STORY LINE: "Someone interacts with someone they love and want and is happily stuck with them in a small space, as a good connection." As a dream symbol, notice the reference to creating a "walled-in" space, which is a clue to the dream's meaning. Together with the story line about happily connecting to someone they deeply love and want, the "enclosed space" image reinforces a pregnancy dream metaphor and message. The dream tells the young woman that she is about to have a child, an experience that she wanted. The handsome dream stranger who she is stuck with in a small space, is a visual announcement about her future son.

EXAMPLE 2 OF FINDING THE STORY LINE: GIVING BIRTH TO SNAKES.

A recently divorced middle-aged woman dreamed that a twenty-five-foot snake was in her backyard and that tiny baby snakes began appearing around her. Then she, herself, began to give birth to hoards of baby snakes; and, they were coming out of the wrong opening of her body, the anus, not where babies normally come from. Hundreds of tiny snakes were being born and she couldn't get them to stop. She felt scared and horrified.

STORY LINE: "Someone sees scary and unwanted items coming at them and out of them and coming out the wrong way, with no control over what is going on." With a divorce, financial problems, and a long list of family troubles, the story line accurately depicted how she was feeling—scared, out of control, and that everything around her was coming out wrong.

EXAMPLE 3 OF FINDING THE STORY LINE: RUNNING ACROSS A WOODEN BRIDGE. A recent college graduate had moved to a new city and had anxieties about finding work in her field. She dreamed she was crossing a rickety old wooden bridge over a dank, green swamp, just for fun, along with her brother and her best friend. At first she was scared because there were eels in the water, but her brother told her it would be okay. The bridge had a few missing planks but the missing pieces were not big enough to fall through and the bridge was stable, so she continued on. Having fun, she began to run back and forth across the bridge. However, as she ran back and forth, the gaps in the planks got wider and wider. They became so large that she had to leap over them. On the last run over the bridge, its end had fallen into the water; to get to safety, she would have to jump into the water and swim to the shore. Feeling terrified, she procrastinated. Her brother tells her that everything will be okay, so she jumps into the water, swims to shore, and is safe.

STORY LINE. "Someone takes greater and greater risks, starting with little ones and going on to larger ones, and despite many challenges, with encouragement, they get to where they want to go." Or, the story could be streamlined to say, "Someone overcomes small and large challenges and ends up okay." As the story line indicates, the dream was a message of encouragement to help her get past the anxiety she was feeling about creating a brand-new life. Using her brother's voice, the dream assured her that it would all work out. As a metaphor, the overall story was saying, "Jump into the water of life; you will not sink."

HOW TO HONE IN ON THE STORY LINE

HINT 1 OF FINDING THE STORY LINE: DO NOT BE DISTRACTED BY SYMBOLS. Many approaches to dream interpretation toss you head-long into a dream's symbol; however, the symbols and background elements can distract from the overall meaning that you seek. To some extent, symbols are the flavoring and décor of a cake, not its substance. Since they carry a lot of the dream's emotional context, symbols *are* important, but first, you examine the story line because it is the plot—embodied in the story line—that most often leads to the message.

HINT 2 OF FINDING THE STORY LINE: HONE IN ON THE PLOT. As you sift through the dream story, focus on the most important actions, reactions, and end results of the dream. As you filter out the bare outline of what is going on, you will begin to see the story line, that like a hidden thread, defines the dream and holds it together.

HINT 3 OF FINDING THE STORY LINE: FOCUS ON THE HEART OF THE MATTER. The story line is a distilled essence of what is most important, including how things turn out. Play with several different one-line descriptions that extract the bare bones of the story, until the one-liner fits. Watch for a shift in your perceptions about the dream as you get to the heart of the subject matter. Do not be satisfied until all the elements of the plot are incorporated into a concise, one line thought.

HINT 4 OF FINDING THE STORY LINE: SUBSTITUTE GENERAL METAPHORS FOR SPECIFIC ACTIONS. A scene of catching a fish can evoke a storyline about someone reaching a goal. A wedding can highlight a story line about someone being ready to make a commitment. Killing an attacker can emphasize an underlying theme about someone defending themselves. You get the drift.

HINT 5 OF FINDING THE STORY LINE: WHAT THE STORY LINE IS NOT. The story line is not an attempt to skip directly to the meaning. It is a way to step back and examine what is going on without getting bogged down by the story's details.

HINT 6 OF FINDING THE STORY LINE: IN A LONG DREAM, CREATE SEVERAL STORY LINES. Sometimes a long dream that has multiple scenes holds a complex message, or it can be several dreams that appear to overlap. Give each section a separate story line. In the end, once you string all the story lines together, they may converge into one coherent message or may turn out to be a series of related messages on a single topic.

When a dream contains a lot of twists and turns and appears to lack a clear, coherent plot, try grouping its similarities and differences. Once you note themes related to what is similar or different, you can convert them into a story line and make headway toward the meaning.

DREAM EXAMPLE 1 OF STORY LINE SIMILARITIES AND DIFFERENCES: THE FRUSTRATED SHOPPER. A woman dreamed she was in a department store shopping for small, everyday beauty products like nail polish, perfume, and mascara. She does not find what she wants and is repeatedly disappointed. Ninety percent of the dream describes rambling scenes of unsuccessful shopping and getting nowhere. In the final scene, which she described almost as an afterthought, the woman finds a beautiful ruby ring that she always wanted. The ring is a perfect fit and is affordable.

What is *similar* in this story, as a story line segment, is that someone repeatedly focuses on the little things in life and fails. What is *different*, as a story line, is that while concentrating on the little things, someone unexpectedly finds a big-ticket item they always wanted. Combining these similar and different elements, *the story line becomes,* "Someone's attempts to chase after the little things in life are difficult and unsuccessful, but by persevering, they find their heart's content." What is the dreamer's heart's content? Whatever she had set as her hopes and goals in life.

When analyzing this dream, almost all of the story was about wandering through stores and not finding items. You could become distracted by those main images and conclude that the story is about someone going around in circles. However, the different ending changed the picture. By contrasting the successful ending to the main action of getting nowhere, the juxtaposition brings the story into focus. When a dream is long and confusing, look for significant differences, similarities, and contrasts and see if that brings out a focal point.

When first attempting to analyze a long dream that rambles, look for a twist in the story that shifts your focus. Such a change in pace or a contrast in a scene can help you notice the main threads of the story and allows the message to jump out.

HINT 8 OF FINDING THE STORY LINE: PRACTICE ON STORIES YOU KNOW. Practice makes perfect. The more dream messages you crack using story lines, the faster you will get at analyzing your dreams. Whether you are stuck in traffic or enjoying a coffee break, try these two-minute practice tricks. Put a story line together in several different versions. Challenge yourself to streamline each version, yet include all the main points that impact the heart of the matter.

PICK A FAIRY TALE. Pretend one of your favorite childhood fairy tales is a dream and find its story line. The gist of "The Ugly Duckling" might be, "Someone is dejected because they do not fit in, yet later discovers their uniqueness and feels overjoyed."

SELECT A MOVIE. Pick a movie that captured your interest. The movie *Gandhi* might have the story line, "Using integrity, courage, and patience, someone who is powerless takes the initiative, and, despite great opposition, brings about enormous positive change." Or the story line for the movie *Titanic* might be, "Faced with desperation and overwhelming odds, both heroism and selfishness emerge."

TELEVISION STORIES. How about a favorite TV program or episode? A game show like *The Price Is Right* might have a story line of, "Some win, some lose, but everyone has a good time." Or the gist for the sitcom *Modern Family* might say, "Where there is love, differences don't matter."

5

A DREAM IS NOT A MINI-MOVIE; IT IS A LINK TO YOUR LIFE

A DREAM SHINES A SPOTLIGHT ON YOUR LIFE. In step two about finding a dream's story line, you extracted the dream's meaning into a story line. In step three, you are checking out where the dream spotlight lands on your life's stage. As we arrive at step three, it is time to realign the extracted story line back into your life. Since the dream is about you, the question becomes, "Where, in my life, or in me, does the story line fit?" Is the story about the inner part of you as a mirror about an attitude, an emotional state, a wish or a goal? Or does the story draw attention to an outer event such a relationship drama, a decision, or a concern about a loved one that tears your heart apart? Step three tells you how to follow the dream's spotlight to re-fit the story line back into your actual life. Once you get that alignment and find where the story matches an area of your life—it often produces an "aha" of meaning. This step can be the most exciting and the most revealing part of the dream analysis! To do so, check out these hints.

STEP THREE: LINKING THE STORY LINE TO YOUR LIFE IS STEP THREE OF THE FIVE-STEP DREAM TECHNIQUE

HINT 1 TO LINK A DREAM TO YOUR LIFE: ASK THE RIGHT QUESTION ABOUT WHAT A DREAM MEANS. As mentioned previously, the question is never "What does this dream mean?" The question is always "To what in me or in my life does the dream refer?" Retaining that focus bears repeating. When you keep in mind that a dream speaks of your life and is not merely an amusing tale, you stay on the right track to finding its meaning. Match the story line to an actual life area or experience, and the meaning surfaces.

HINT 2 TO LINK A DREAM TO YOUR LIFE: THE IMPORTANCE OF MATCHING THE STORY LINE TO AN AREA OF YOUR LIFE. As if moving a puzzle piece around a board to see how it fits, scan your life to see where the story line coincides with an attitude, a relationship, activity, or an ongoing situation. *For example*, suppose you dream that you ran a race in the Olympics and won a gold medal. The story line says, "After much effort, someone succeeds brilliantly" or, "By persevering, someone achieves great things." Which success in your life is highlighted by the dream, depends on your life; only you can know what that success is for you. To some it may refer to fitting into a glamorous outfit after losing weight; to others it might be completing a degree or sprinting up the corporate ladder.

HINT 3 TO LINK A DREAM TO YOUR LIFE: TURN THE STORY LINE INTO A QUESTION. If you have trouble fitting a story line to an area of your life, try turning it into a question.

DREAM EXAMPLE 1 OF TURNING A STORY LINE INTO QUESTIONS: INVADING MY SPACE. A man dreams of walking into his office and seeing the manager's assistant at his desk pulling off pieces of Scotch tape for her own use. She has no right to be in his office or go through his belongings. He walks up to her and asks her in a quiet voice, "What are you doing?" She knows she has been caught doing something off limits but ignores him and blatantly defies him by continuing to rip off tape. The man stays quiet and does not challenge her further because he is not sure what to do. *The story line is,* "Someone watches another misuse their position but does not know how to stop them." The story line calls to mind questions like: Where in your life is someone overstepping their boundaries? Are you letting someone take advantage of you? Is there a situation at work or elsewhere in your life, where you would like to speak up but feel unsafe to do so? As you answer the questions that the story line initiates, the life area that the dream relates to should become clear.

DREAM EXAMPLE 2 OF TURNING A STORY LINE INTO QUESTIONS: THE WOUND. A dreamer is shocked to see a large, gaping wound dripping with blood. *The story line is,* "Someone sees something that needs a lot of help." This story line begs these questions: Where in your life do you feel wounded or in pain? Have you overlooked someone around you who may be hurting? Have you, or someone close to you, caused emotional damage by your actions or habits?

DREAM EXAMPLE 3 OF TURNING A STORY LINE INTO QUESTIONS: A BEAUTIFUL SCARF. A woman dreams that her work associates are frantic and scurrying to get things done. She ignores them and peacefully puts on a wide, red silk scarf, carefully tying a bow in an artistic arrangement. *The story line is,* "Instead of getting caught up in the frenzy and chaos around her, someone peacefully focuses on creating something beautiful." The story line brings up questions like: In what area of your life are others frantic? Would concentrating on doing your best resolve an issue? Are there creative activities that would distract you from the anxieties in your life?

HINT 4 TO LINK A DREAM TO YOUR LIFE: THE STORY LINE MAY RELATE TO YOUR INNER OR OUTER LIFE. As you search for answers raised by story line questions, insights about a particular situation in your life may begin to pop up. When matching a story line to an area of your life, remember that you lead two lives: an inner one and an outer one. Sometimes the life event about which the dream is commenting is an attitude, an emotion, a set of thoughts, or a perspective that is going on *within* you. Your inner life is also subject to lots of episodes and events, so to speak. We tend to look at outside circumstances and events for the meaning of a dream, but just as often, a dream relates to your character, attitudes, or thoughts about potential decisions, hopes, fears, and wishes.

6

SYMBOLS AND DREAMS

HIP HIP, HURRAY, FOR DREAM SYMBOLS.
After relegating symbols to second place during step
one of the Five-Step Dream Technique, in step four,
we return, full circle, to examine the importance of dream symbols and dream characters. The story line gives you a template
for the dream's overall meaning. Now, you can place a dream
symbol into that template to clarify and enhance the dream's
meaning.

Symbols are also a critical bridge, providing a link between
several dream factors. *First*, a symbol is a link between a past
memory and a current life event, and reveals how the past and
present overlap. *Second*, because of its association to a past experience, a symbol is a direct links to your emotions. How the symbol
impacts your feelings can color the message and have a major effect
on the meaning of the dream. *Third*, because of its link to your

memory, a symbol is also a link to your unconscious mind, the hidden part of you that stores forgotten experiences, wishes, goals and even repressed traumas. Like finding a buried treasure chest, a dream symbol can unearth a wealth of feelings and discoveries about yourself and your past. As you see how the past has shaped you with the help of a dream symbol, you become more free to choose your future path. In step four, we re-establish the amazing and transformative role that a dream symbol can play, and see how to get to the meaning of a dream symbol.

STEP FOUR: EXAMINING THE SYMBOLS IS STEP FOUR OF THE FIVE-STEP DREAM TECHNIQUE

THREE MAIN WAYS TO FIND THE MEANING OF A DREAM SYMBOL.
Explore the following well-established approaches of finding the meaning of a dream symbol; a detailed description of each approach follows. As you try out various methods on your dreams, you will notice that the selection of symbols by your psyche is anything but random! The mind works hard to select a specific symbol, to convey a precise message.

FREUD'S PAST ASSOCIATIONS METHOD. Take a symbol backward in time to a past memory or an experience and relate the past tidbit to the current dream story, and to a current life situation.

JUNG'S PARALLEL ASSOCIATIONS. Explore what a dream symbol means to you now, as its current meanings, for you.

FRITZ PERL'S "BECOME THE SYMBOL" APPROACH. This is a dramatic role-playing technique. You experience a symbol or a main dream character by engaging in a pretend conversation with it. As you let yourself become the symbol, you bypass the logical mind and intuit the symbol's hidden undercurrents.

FREUD: LINK A DREAM SYMBOL TO YOUR PAST. In working with the dreams of his patients, Freud noticed that dream symbols related to their past experiences, ones that had an emotional impact on the dreamer. To investigate the meaning of their symbols, he instructed clients to go back in time to those past memories and, as they lay on a couch, he let them dredge up their past associations about their symbols. As such memories surfaced, Freud linked their memories to the dream symbol, which could be either an object or a person. This "going backward in time" effect is like a magician pulling a long scarf out of a sleeve—a host of colorful memories pop out.

Following a dream symbol to its past origins is easier than it sounds. Suppose you dream of a child's sled. Think of the last time you saw or experienced a sled. Did you have a sled as a child? See a sled in a store window? Read about a sled or notice a red sled in a movie scene? Review what were you doing, thinking, or feeling when you experienced the sled and see if that memory connects to what is happening now, as a dream-related issue. If something clicks, examine how that memory might shed light on current circumstances related to the dream.

DREAM EXAMPLE 1: THE COLOR YELLOW. In his real life, a man walked out on his wife. On the last day that he was at home, his wife wore a yellow dress. A few months later the man's dreams began to fill with the color yellow. The yellow hue became connected to leaving his wife, and became a connection, for him, of sorrow and sadness. Because negative feelings can tie you up in knots and spiral into depression, the color yellow became a message about dealing with his marriage, or at least dealing with his feelings. To avoid depression, drinking, or other self-destructive behaviors, repeated dreams about the color yellow urged him to either make peace with his wife or deal with the pain of the breakup.

DREAM EXAMPLE 2: THE BASEBALL GAME. A middle-aged man dreamed of playing baseball and scoring a home run with a special bat. Taking the game of baseball as a dream symbol, he remembered how he loved to play baseball in his youth and how he had achieved a high batting average at neighborhood games. The story line said, "Something someone loves doing used a special tool and brings success."

For this middle-aged dreamer, his baseball memories were associations of doing what he loved. This reminder of his past led him to admit how dissatisfied he was at work. In his view, he did the lion's share of work at his company yet received the smallest slice of the corporate pie. Recent frustrations had him toying with the idea of using his amazing skill of building trust with customers to start his own business. Freud's method of examining past memories associated with a dream symbol had unearthed feelings of satisfaction that he once had, playing baseball. Those memories prompted him to believe in himself again, as he had in his youth. Putting the pieces together, the man took the plunge and went on to start his own business, with no regrets.

SUMMARY OF FREUD'S METHOD: FOLLOW A DREAM SYMBOL INTO ITS PAST. To Freud, a dream symbol is a picture that jogs your memory about something in your past, and those past memories shed light on a message that relates to the present. The more you try this technique, the more you'll love it.

- Pick a dream symbol that has a strong effect on you or that mystifies you.

- Review events and feelings that the symbol brings up from your past.

- Explore how those past memories (as direct memories or as metaphors) and the wordplay around those memories, shed light on a current issue.

- Keep going backward in time until something from the past clicks and brings meaning to the current issue. The past link may not click immediately, but there is always a past link.

CARL JUNG: WHAT A DREAM SYMBOL MEANS TO YOU TODAY. Jung noted that your current thoughts about a dream symbol may also contribute to the meaning of the dream. If you dream of a lake, instead of remembering a past experience at a lake, think of what a lake means to you now, in general. Images may come to mind of relaxation or a vacation getaway. Or, seeing an athlete in a dream may remind you of going to the gym, or may relate a goal to optimize your health.

Any dream symbol can have dual associations—one from the past and a current one—and keeping an eye on both can be useful. To explore more of Jung's thoughts about symbols and dreams, check out his memoire, *Memories, Dreams, Reflections*. Though riveting, it is not a light read.

FRITZ PERLS: BECOME THE DREAM SYMBOL. Psychologist Fritz Perls encouraged dreamers to become a dream character or symbol. This exercise can be acted out by putting two chairs face-to-face. One chair represents the dreamer, the other the dream character, and you move back and forth between chairs, acting out each role. This also works as a written dialogue.

Though becoming a dream character can sound childish or strange—it works, especially for dreams where the logical mind fails to grasp the message. As a playful, non-intellectual exercise, this approach allows blocked thoughts and feelings to come forward. As you merge with a symbol and open the doors of your unconscious, you may intuit the metaphors that escape logic. When all else fails or even as a fun exercise, try Fritz Perl's method on a symbol that makes no sense. The results may surprise you.

DREAM EXAMPLE: WHAT IS THIS RAT DOING IN MY LIVING ROOM? A fun demonstration of becoming a symbol happened at a seminar. At the urging of his girlfriend, an important head of a corporation attended a dream class. Even though he was skeptical about the usefulness of dreams, as a good sport, the man shared his dream about an arrogant rat. In the dream, he was very upset that a rat had invaded his living room, leaving a gaping hole in the wall behind a beautiful sofa. When he tried to shoo the rat away in the dream, the creature puffed up its chest and stood in the middle of the living room as if it owned the place. The dream annoyed and perplexed the handsome executive.

Becoming the symbol works well for a dream that evokes intense feelings, like the anger that this dreamer felt. After two chairs were placed in the middle of the room face-to-face, the executive began to role play—himself versus the rat. He asked, "Rat, what are you doing in the middle of my living room? How dare you take over my space?" Moving into the other chair, he paused to compose the arrogant rodent's reply and his facial expression turned into wide-eyed shock. As participants looked on with curiosity, the company president doubled over with laughter then explained what had happened. As the head of a company, he was used to getting his own way with employees, even when it made them uncomfortable. As soon as he sat in the rat's chair, the executive realized that *he* was the arrogant rat. Though the man was not always full of himself, the dream invited him to note his occasional arrogance and deal with it. To the executive's credit and a tip of the hat to his dream, the man softened his stance and improved his leadership style.

HINTS ABOUT DREAM SYMBOLS:
ALL YOU NEED TO KNOW

HINT 1 ABOUT DREAM SYMBOLS: DREAM SYMBOLS COMMUNICATE LIKE A GAME OF CHARADES. In the parlor game Charades, one person silently acts out a word or a phrase while others try to guess what they are acting out. As such, Charades is an "image-to-word" association game. For example, in Charades, circling your hand around your ear, and leaning forward as if you are listening to something, conveys the nonverbal, metaphoric message to players that your word "sounds like" another word. In the same way, dream symbols pantomime a visual metaphor. Dream symbols use a silent, visual image to convey a related message. Once you approach dream symbols as a playful pantomime like Charades, their messages begin to pop open.

HINT 2 ABOUT DREAM SYMBOLS: SYMBOLS ARE A PRECISE SELECTION. A dream symbol can seem like a random selection. A question people often ask is, "I saw a striped blue shirt in a store window yesterday and last night I dreamed about it. Is that just a coincidence?" The answer is no, it is not a coincidence. Whether the blue shirt is a memory from yesterday or a memory from ten years ago, the psyche selects it as a specific symbol from your memory storage, to communicate a precise message.

For example, as the man glanced at the blue shirt in the store window, the thought crossed his mind that his boss had a similar shirt, and it occurred to him that he would look good in that shirt, too. Like a domino effect, his observation brought up the thought of working toward a promotion. In that instant, the blue shirt became paired to his ambitions and became a symbol of achieving success. Once career advancement was on his mind and linked to the store window shirt, the dream featuring the blue shirt became feedback that he was on the right track in dusting off his ambitions. That's the way dream symbols work, and that's the way they are selected— because of their associations to your thoughts, feelings, memories, and experiences.

Once upon a time, dreams were considered accidental mini-movies, which, like a slip of the tongue by the unconscious, popped up unannounced as you slept. In the modern view, the mind applies predictable rules to communicate an insight via a dream and works hard to get a message across. Experience in dream analysis now indicates that the psyche's choice of a symbol to convey a message is anything but random. As fantastic as it may seem to some, the selection of a dream symbol aligns both the emotional and the intellectual parts of a conveyed message. The mind is still the greatest computer ever.

HINT 3 ABOUT DREAM SYMBOLS: SYMBOLS ARE THE ICING, NOT THE CAKE. Though at times a symbol can, in and of itself, be the entire dream message, in most cases, a dream symbol is the backup singer, not the lead. More often a symbol is the icing on the cake that adds flavor and depth to a dream. Like a 3D visual image, a dream symbol is a link between your past experience and a current circumstance, a link that, when explored, opens up deeper insights. Playing a backup role does not make a dream symbol any less important. After all, what's a cake without a sweet topping?

HINT 4 ABOUT DREAM SYMBOLS: TO BETTER UNDERSTAND A SYMBOL, UNPLUG YOUR MIND. Instead of concentrating on a dream symbol as if you are taking a test when looking for its meaning, adopt a playful attitude. A relaxed focus lets you sail into the creative parts of your own brain—a creative state during which the links of past experience that relate to a symbol can breeze through.

HINT 5 ABOUT DREAM SYMBOLS: SYMBOLS AND THE METAPHORS THEY CREATE ARE UNIQUE, INDIVIDUAL MESSAGES. Dream symbols are selected from your personal experience (your memories) to concoct a message tailored specifically for you, and only for you. If you were in a motorcycle accident and you later dream about a motorcycle, because the motorcycle is a reference to the accident, as a dream symbol it signals danger, fear, or distress. However, if you joined a bike club and love the camaraderie of group rides, dreaming of a motorcycle can be a message about good connections, fun, and adventure. Or, dreaming of a daisy may remind one woman of the fields where she grew up, as a message about early family values. However, a bouquet of daisies may remind another woman of flowers she saw in a store window as a young woman and could never afford, as a message about feeling deprived. Though it is the exact same symbol—a daisy, each receives a different message because of their individual memories of that symbol. As you ponder your dream symbols, trust your experience and review your memories about the symbol. Once you see how easily a dream image connects with your own experience, understanding dream symbols will be as natural as getting the punch line of a joke.

HINT 6 ABOUT DREAM SYMBOLS: SYMBOLS MIRROR YOUR COMMUNICATION STYLE. Notice how you express yourself. If you are a polite communicator, your dream characters will have manners. If you are poetic and like to elaborate, your dream scenes and symbols will be detailed and profuse. One lady in a dream group was a writer. Her dreams were a three-act flourish sporting an introduction, a main scene, and a conclusion. The hero in her dreams was easy to spot and her plots were worthy of a Hollywood production. The dreams of an accountant who rarely spoke were short and often included numbers. For extra insight on deciphering your dream symbols, check your communication style.

HINT 7 ABOUT DREAM SYMBOLS: SYMBOLS CAN BE A PLAY ON WORDS OR IMAGES. As visual metaphors, symbols often engage playfulness and a sense of humor, as in these examples.

- *A swimming seal.* Shiny black seals somersaulting in the water may denote a seal on an envelope or be a play on words for "sealing a deal."

- *An insect* can act as a metaphor for something that bugs you.

- *A clock that runs* out the door is a visual symbol for time running out.

- *A huge head* can reference conceit and egotism.

- *A bathroom* is a metaphor for a place to cleanse or to seek relief.

- *Looking for a bathroom* can be about wanting to release or letting go of crap.

- *A house or room* can symbolize expanding opportunities or new horizons.

- *Driving* is a visual metaphor for learning to maneuver or for something that moves you forward.

SHARED DREAM SYMBOLS: A SYMBOL CAN MEAN THE SAME THING TO A GROUP OF PEOPLE

AT TIMES, DREAM SYMBOLS CAN HAVE THE SAME MEANING FOR MANY. Some dream symbols bring up similar memories for many, such as the Statue of Liberty as a symbol of freedom and of a new life for the many who entered the United States as immigrants. A shared symbol can be a flag that evokes patriotism, or can be a specific object such as Big Ben, a clock that evokes cultural memories of London, England, or it can be an iconic figure such as Superman, a symbol of heroic action. Such group or cultural symbols carry the same meaning for everyone in a group or society. As electronics widen our world, we recognize and relate to increasing numbers of icons and shared symbols.

PERSONAL AND SHARED DREAM SYMBOLS CAN INTERACT. At times, there can be an interplay between an individual and a shared symbol.

For example, a gold cross on a chain can be a personal symbol as a gift from a deceased grandmother. In a dream, it may remind you that you are loved. However, if you dream of a cross during a crisis, as a shared religious symbol, the same cross may signal a need to look to your spiritual roots for strength.

EXAMPLES OF SYMBOLS WITH SHARED MEANINGS. Even though most dream symbols relate to individual memories, it helps to note a few common associations. These examples describe *common stereotypes* that sometimes come into play in an individual's dream.

ANIMALS. We laugh at photos of people who resemble their pets, and in dreams, an animal is a convenient stereotype for a person's traits. A snoozing kitty may hint at a need for rest or highlight a lethargic patch in your life, a dog can mirror loyalty or friendship, an eagle may suggest keen perception, and a fox can indicate cleverness.

CARS AND VEHICLES. A car may, on occasion, represent your body, since a car, like your body, is a vessel or vehicle that carries you through life. Seeing mechanical problems in the car may be a heads-up to check your health, or to have your car checked. Watching a car in motion in a dream may relate to reaching a goal or symbolize a need to get somewhere, or to move along. Or a dream about a sexy sports car might represent a young man's emerging charm.

CHILDREN. Children in dreams can denote a variety of messages. A young child can depict innocence or indicate immature behavior. Since a child has unlimited potential yet requires care and attention, a child can be a metaphor for a new project or opportunity that requires a long-term commitment. How the child fares in the dream can hint at how a related project is doing.

CLOTHES. You change clothes to suit your mood, to suit weather, or to live up to roles in life such as a well-dressed businessman or a bohemian artist. Since garments mirror your activities and emotions, clothes in a dream often symbolize your attitudes. Someone who is shy may see themselves wearing a bold red color as an invitation to step into the limelight. A heavy coat may denote a need to feel protected, while a light summer dress can express a studious dreamer's need to lighten up.

DEATH AND DYING. For many, death is the biggest change we can possibly encounter, and because of that, death in dreams is often a symbol for drastic change. Since many of us fear death, images of dying and destruction can also relate to intense fears. Though almost all dreams about death are metaphors, on rare occasions a dream about death can be a literal warning. Such dreams tend to be more intense and literal in content, and as warnings, they are often repeated.

FACES AND FEATURES. Body parts such as a face, arms, or feet are often linked to their activity. Teeth may relate to how you communicate. Rotting or decayed teeth can hint that communications need mending. An ear can relate to listening habits, while feet and legs can reference your path in life. Since hair and thoughts emerge from the head, hair and scalp may symbolize what is on your mind. Sores or bugs on the scalp can be a metaphor for painful or negative thoughts, or attitudes that need attention or warrant change.

MONEY, JEWELS, PURSES, HANDBAGS, AND WALLETS. When money, jewels, valuables, or an item that holds your valuables appear in a dream, their appearance may be a symbolic question about what you value in life. Or, such images may invite you to examine your attitude toward your possessions.

ROOMS AND SPECIFIC LOCATIONS. Dreams about a room or a specific location can relate to whatever goes on in that room. An airport can refer to rising above an issue or mirror an attempt to reach a goal. A tennis court can bring up questions about how you play tennis or about how you "play ball" with others, as a metaphor for cooperation. A kitchen can relate to eating habits or may be a metaphor for what you are cooking up in life. Dreaming about a bedroom can speak of relationships, passion, or a need for rest.

7

LIGHTS, CAMERA, ACTION: ARRIVING AT THE DREAM MESSAGE

CROSSING THE FINISH LINE IN A DREAM ANALYSIS. Even though step five of the Five-Step Dream Technique is the official point at which you arrive at the dream message, often the dream's meaning pops out during step two, three or four. Great. But what if you get to step five and still have no idea what the dream means? Or, what if y ou think you know the meaning of the dream but do not feel comfortable about what to do with it? How can you be sure of the dream message and how to apply an insight with confidence? This section covers both eventualities—what to do if the message still escapes your attention, and how to use a message in a practical way. The chapter ends with five examples of actual dreams, their meaning, and how the message applies to the dreamer's life.

STEP FIVE: DECIDING ON THE MEANING OF A DREAM IS STEP FIVE OF THE FIVE-STEP DREAM TECHNIQUE

HINT 1: SEE IF THE SHOE FITS. Coming to understand a dream's message can, at first, be like shopping for shoes. As you trek through possibilities at a shoe store, you see what catches your eye, try on a few styles and sizes, then see what fits. In the same way, finding the dream message begins as a "trying on" exercise as you trek through the Five-Step Dream Technique. You start by naming the emotions and then you create a story line, link the story line to an area of your life, and then examine the main dream symbols. As you browse through each step and the possible meanings it brings up, somewhere along the way, you arrive at an initial fit.

HINT 2: IF BY STEP FIVE, THE MEANING OF THE DREAM STILL FEELS ELUSIVE, TRY AGAIN. By step five, a clear understanding of the dream message should have surfaced. However, if the dream still does *not* evoke a clear "aha" moment, explore these options.

TRY AGAIN, OPTION 1: A NEW STORY LINE. Try putting new and different words to the story line. Since the story line is a key ingredient, its one-line wording and gist must be a bull's-eye, or it must at least hit the target. The story line is often the sticking point.

TRY AGAIN, OPTION 2: THE DREAM-TO-LIFE LINK. Sometimes the sticking point is how you connected the dream to an area of your life. Though most dreams are about you, on rare occasions a dream can be about someone close to you such as a friend or family member, a colleague, or even an issue like a sports event or a political outcome. Try broadening the scope of where the story line may fit into your life as a puzzle piece. Who or what situation "sounds like" the dream's story line? To churn the brain in the direction of broader options, check out the twenty-seven dream types logged by the author at InterpretADream.com

TRY AGAIN, OPTION 3: MOVE ON. If playing with several versions of the story line does not do the trick, and matching it to an area of life does not produce a click about the dream's meaning, put the dream aside for a few days or weeks. Sometimes the passage of time lets you dusts off a fresh perspective about a puzzling dream and later leads to the message.

HINT 3: BY USING DREAM INSIGHTS, CLEAR DREAMS KEEP COMING. Because of busy lifestyles, even your spouse or best friend hears only a small sliver of what you really think and feel. The exception is your psyche, the part of your mind that is aware of all you think, feel, and do. By sending you nightly dream memos, your psyche acts like a best friend and inner voice; when you apply the insight, you acknowledge its helpfulness and the dreams keep coming. If you ask a friend for advice and then ignore it, the friend clams up. The same can happen with dream advice. However, unlike your friend, the psyche does not give up. Unless you choose to set your dreams aside, as your inner voice, the psyche will repeat a message and reinstate a dialogue whenever you are ready.

Once you have an interpretation that rings true, record the message you received, along with the dream. The insight may invite you to work on an attitude, improve a talent, take a step in your career, mend a relationship, or review your options about a decision. An insight may suggest that you think before you speak, or look up what career training is available. The time may arrive when you will want to review your dreams, which could be years later. If you record the insight along with the dream, you will be glad to note the gems that reveal your progress through life.

HINT 5: APPLY THE MESSAGE IN A PRACTICAL WAY. Unless you are in a dire situation that warrants extreme advice, guidance from dreams is rarely drastic in nature. Dreams are stories about you and your life, stories that convey practical insights. Their messages are consistent with your beliefs and lifestyle and are intended to lead you into natural and positive change. Whether a dream story is goofy, uplifting, or scary, the intention behind its message is always to help. And more important, the message is *practical*.

For example, a scene about the end of the world is not a call to stash food and water into a bunker; instead, its message says, "Life as I know it, is ending," a common scene for teens who are dipping a toe into adulthood. And unless you live in an earthquake-prone area, earthquakes are a great metaphor for "your life is being turned upside down," a message frequently seen in dreams of those going through a divorce or an unexpected financial crisis.

No matter what the image or story, as a thought from your inner self, dreams give down-to-earth advice that should bring more harmony, success, and understanding into your life, rather than disrupt it.

HINT 6: EXTREME SCENES TELL YOU SOMETHING. Since dream messages are supposed to be practical and positive, people wonder why scenes are often drastic. Extreme images appear for several reasons.

EXTREME SCENE, REASON 1: YOU ARE NOT LISTENING. Like a loud knock at your door, dreams often exaggerate to get your attention. At times it can take an intense scene for you to remember a dream.

EXTREME SCENE, REASON 2: THE MESSAGE IS VERY IMPORTANT. The more important the message, the harder your psyche tries to get through to your awareness. Sometimes an extreme or a frightening scene is the equivalent of a loud shout to flag the dream's importance.

EXTREME SCENE, REASON 3: A SENSITIVE TOPIC. The dream may broach a touchy subject that makes you react. The more intense your feelings are about a topic, the more you may try to push the dream away. Such a "push-back effect" is the equivalent of donning dark glasses. When you view an object or a scene through a dark lens, it can look scary, turning a normal dream into images that appear more extreme. The dream itself is not scary; however, your reactions to the topic turn it into a scary episode.

EXTREME SCENE, REASON 4: YOU MISUNDERSTAND THE DREAM'S INTENTION. Have you ever seen a movie scene of a woman running through a garage at night, chased by a shadowy figure who is shouting at her? The woman is terrified, but when the shadowy figure catches up, she discovers it is the night watchman with the car keys she dropped at the door as she left. Some extreme dream scenes are like that—a misunderstanding about the intentions of the dream messenger and its message.

HINT 7: DREAM MESSAGES NORMALLY CREATE A SLOW PACE OF CHANGE. Insights from dreams tend to create tiny shifts in your attitudes, personality, or career steps. Once in a while, a dream may initiate a huge shift by presenting an instant solution to a problem that has been haunting you. However, most changes evoked by dreams are as imperceptible as a flower that unfolds in graceful silence. You hardly notice the effect until, one day, you look back and notice an increase in confidence, improved relationships, and greater satisfaction at work, which, if you look closely, you might attribute to dream guidance.

HINT 8: BE CONFIDENT IN YOUR ANALYSIS. Be confident in your ability to decipher your dreams! If you want to compare an analysis of a particular dream, look up similar dreams that were analyzed by experts. At InterpretADream.com you can use keywords to search an e-library of dreams on a wide range of topics, or request an expert's opinion about an unusual dream.

FIVE EXAMPLE DREAMS OF HOW A DREAM INSIGHT COMES TOGETHER

Here are a few examples of actual dreams and their practical messages, obtained using the Five-Step Dream Technique. Dreamers from around the globe e-mailed dreams to the author at InterpretADream .com, requesting a free sample that is offered on the site. The dreams represent a cross-section of content and issues. Notice that the story line is what guides and prompts the direction of the message.

Example 1 of a Dream Analysis: Lion Attacks Spouse.

This dream shows strong emotional content. Notice how the ending is a hint about how things turn out.

THE DREAMER: A woman in an African country, age 32.

THE DREAM: We are sitting outside on chairs. My husband's chair is facing me and he is sitting next to my uncle. I see a lion approach and tell my uncle and husband to move, but they ignore me. The lion spares my uncle but lunges at my husband and attacks his head. My uncle tries to help, but he cannot. I scream and find a stick to hit the lion on the head and make it leave. My husband is unconscious, but he survives. I see other lions that are not harming us, but I'm still afraid.

MAIN LIFE ISSUES: Husband is sick and there are fears for his business and health.

HOW I FELT: Scared.

THE STORY LINE: Though intensely threatened, someone manages to save the day.

MAIN SYMBOLS

LION: Danger; that which frightens.

STICK: A weapon; what saves the day.

THE MESSAGE: Seeing lions in the distance mirrors your fears about your husband's health and earnings. Because the lions in the distance do not hurt you, his business and income will be fine. The direct attack by a lion on your husband relates to your anxiety about his illness. However, in the dream, you rescue your husband and the lion leaves. This tells you he will recover.

BOTTOM LINE: The end of a dream often shows how things turn out. In your dream, your husband survives because you came to his aid. Do all you can and he will be fine.

Example 2 of a Dream Analysis: Texting Problems.

Notice how, in this dream, the images and actions repeat. The repetitions show the sense of urgency experienced by the dreamer and an urgency about the issues addressed by the dream.

THE DREAMER: Adult, age 41.

THE DREAM: I am trying to text, e-mail, or call someone, but no matter how hard I try, I can't hit the right buttons on my cell phone. My fingers just can't find the right buttons.

MAIN LIFE ISSUES: Changes in work and personal life.

HOW I FELT: Frustrated.

THE STORY LINE: Someone's efforts to connect with others do not work.

MAIN SYMBOLS

PHONE: A communication tool.

CAN'T HIT THE RIGHT BUTTONS: Suggests confusion and anxiety.

FINGERS DO NOT WORK: Lost skills or ineffective actions.

THE MESSAGE: The dream suggests that communications with others are not working. It indirectly hints that your problem may best be resolved by backing off and learning to communicate, instead of continuing to do what you are doing.

BOTTOM LINE: You may want to rethink how you communicate and see if there is room for improvement. The images suggest you may be trying too hard and that you keep doing what is ineffective. Sometimes less is more. Staying silent and displaying self-control can at times achieve more than shouting or long conversations. If you are having trouble communicating, it may be important to calm down.

Example 3 of a Dream Analysis: Chased by a Big Dog.

In this dream, all the images center around a common theme of feeling scared and overwhelmed, which is then used in the story line.

THE DREAMER: Teenager, age 16.

THE DREAM: I'm outside of my house with my mother, father, and sister. We are having a barbecue and it is a beautiful day. All of a sudden my family freezes, stops what they are doing, and everyone goes back inside the house, acting like robots. I am the only person left outside. As the sky begins to darken, I try to go into the house but it feels as if gravity holds me down and I can't move. I fall to the ground and begin to crawl. As I crawl, a huge black dog comes out of the backyard. As the dog gets closer, I crawl faster, but the front door seems to move farther away. I try to scream but no noise comes out. The dog gets close but I can't move. I stop and when I look in the dog's direction, it is right on top of me and I wake up.

MAIN LIFE ISSUES: Stress from school and the drama around me.

HOW I FELT: Scared.

THE STORY LINE: Someone feels vulnerable and has trouble moving forward.

MAIN SYMBOLS:

FAMILY BARBECUE: Happy events with loved ones.

CAN'T MOVE: Feeling stuck.

BIG BLACK DOG: What feels threatening; what frightens.

CAN'T SCREAM: Having no voice; not feeling heard.

THE MESSAGE: Wanting to scream and not being able to do so suggests that you feel you do not have a voice in life and that you may have trouble communicating what you need and what you want. Running from the dog indicates that you feel vulnerable and overwhelmed. It can help to talk to a family member or a counselor who can give you hints about how to build up coping mechanisms to handle life's daily challenges.

BOTTOM LINE: At age sixteen, life can feel intense, mysterious, and overwhelming, but in time, you will figure it out.

Example 4 of a Dream Analysis: The Arm Tattoo.

When you see something new, different, and startling in a dream, as happens in this dream, it is often an invitation to do something new or to reach for a fresh perspective. In the dream, the central symbol plays a key role in determining the message.

THE DREAMER: Man, age 29.

THE DREAM: In real life I have no tattoos, yet I dreamed that I had a tattoo on my left forearm. The image was a God figure and I was annoyed, confused, and wondering how it got there. As I looked closer, I noticed that the God-like figure was holding a spear.

MAIN LIFE ISSUES: Recognition, being underestimated. People tend to forget about my presence, especially at work.

HOW I FELT: Annoyed.

THE STORY LINE: Someone is surprised to see an unexpected visual item permanently placed in a personal location that is visible to others.

MAIN SYMBOLS:

TATTOO: Often a macho symbol. Also can be a way of one's highlighting beliefs or personal strengths and making them visible to others.

GOD FIGURE: A symbol of spirituality and beliefs beyond oneself.

SPEAR: A tool for survival. Also a symbol of masculinity.

THE MESSAGE: The symbol of God as a tattoo suggests that the answer to finding your strength and becoming more visible may be found by defining your spiritual path and making your beliefs more known to others. A spear is a warrior's tool. The image hints that you may have issues related to asserting yourself and a need to speak up.

BOTTOM LINE: People who connect to something greater than themselves, such as God and spiritual beliefs, tend to be more confident. As a result of their confidence, they exude more presence in a group. The dream suggests that defining your spirituality will help you gain strength and confidence, which in turn can help you assert yourself in a constructive manner, so that you no longer feel invisible to others.

Example 5 of a Dream Analysis:
My Brothers Try to Kill Me.

Many dreams appear illogical and disjointed, like this one, with unexpected people popping up out of nowhere and U-turns in the plot. Starting your analysis by finding the story line allows you to unify what is going on and not be distracted by the sudden changes in imagery.

THE DREAMER: Woman, age 43.

THE DREAM: My brothers were trying to kill me near my apartment. I ran from them, got home, put my disabled boyfriend into a wheelchair, and called 9-1-1. I told them that the devil was there to kill me. As I talked on the phone, I ran outside and down the street. The police arrived and picked me up, then we went back to my apartment. My boyfriend was not hurt and I was okay.

MAIN LIFE ISSUES: Family, issues with brothers, and work challenges.

HOW I FELT: Fearful.

THE STORY LINE: Though under attack, someone protects self and loved ones.

MAIN SYMBOLS:

RUNNING: Under attack.

TRYING TO KILL ME: Metaphor for feeling threatened, or for others trying to force their views on another or to force change on the dreamer.

CALL 9-1-1: Seeking help in a traditional way; getting the law on your side.

THE POLICE ARRIVE: Law and order is restored; getting back one's power.

THE MESSAGE: Dreams exaggerate to make a point, so the attacks likely symbolize the verbal fights that are probably taking place during family feuds. Running indicates that the family fights make you feel vulnerable. However, the end of the dream shows that all ends well. The ending indicates that you will handle the challenges and prevail.

BOTTOM LINE: Do what you know is right and all will work out.

8

ADVANCED DREAM ANALYSIS HINTS

TAKING A LEAP IN DREAM UNDERSTANDING. Like any other skill that you master, the more proficient you become, the more you notice how a tool can be applied or expressed. The same is true with interpreting your dreams. As you establish a dialogue with your psyche and become more comfortable with the messages you receive, you begin to notice more. Some insights can be fun, like noticing that your psyche has a sense of humor and embeds a joke into a dream message once in a while. Other insights can be startling, like discovering that your psyche begins to "teach" you how to understand your dreams, akin to the private signals that a couple silently exchanges across a crowded room. As you begin to enjoy the sport of understanding your life through dreams, your understanding of dreams will expand. Like an Olympic champion, you flex your muscles and dive deeper. Although this chapter cannot cover the full range of advanced topics or questions about dream analysis, it offers a few ideas that should satisfy even the most daring. Enjoy.

ADVANCED DREAM ANALYSIS HINTS

ADVANCED HINT # 1: YOU OFTEN FIND ADVICE AT THE END OF A DREAM. Although an entire dream can produce insights, specific suggestions about what to do next often appear at the end. Check how a dream ends to see what may resonate as advice.

DREAM EXAMPLE: THE TARANTULA AND THE GUARD. Faced with rumors that his company was downsizing, a young man feared he might lose his job. He dreamed he was at a train station, lying down in the middle of the tracks as trains zoomed by without harming him. As he lay peacefully on a white blanket, a huge black tarantula above his head caught his eye. Feeling afraid and in danger, the man ran for help. He found a guard and pointed to the tarantula. As they watched, a train came by and crushed the tarantula. The guard turned to the young man and said, "There is no problem now," and walked away. In the end, the danger disappeared as suddenly as it had arrived. The ending suggested that despite rumors about downsizing, the young man's job was safe and he was not in danger.

Notice a dream's final images. If you see someone in a terrible storm yet they find a safe haven, all will be well. Or suppose you witness a car crash, which might be a metaphor of a major clash or fight with a loved one. If at the end of the dream, no one is harmed and all is well, whatever the disagreement, peace will be restored.

ADVANCED HINT # 2: TIME MARKERS IN DREAMS—WHEN WILL SOMETHING HAPPEN? Dreams often portray probabilities, and an occasional ESP dream gives you a glimpse into the future. Yet such dreams seldom specify *when* an event will take place. Time markers in dreams are rare, but if they *do* appear, the predicted timing tends to be accurate.

For example, a woman dreams of meeting her true love. The first question that pops into her head is "When?" and the answer is that no one knows. She may cross paths with a future love in a few months or in a few years; unless a dream provides a time marker, there is no way for her to know. An example of a timing marker would be a dream about a wedding that shows a current friend of the bride, as a bridesmaid. In the dream, the bridesmaid just turned thirty, which tells the prospective bride that she will marry when her friend turns thirty. Or, a time marker may show the date on a wedding announcement. Though rare, keep an eye out for timing markers in dreams.

ADVANCED HINT # 3: SPOKEN WORDS IN DREAMS ARE OFTEN LITERAL. Dreams are visual metaphors, yet paradoxically, when words are spoken in a dream, their meaning is often literal. If a relative tells you to see a doctor, you should make an appointment. If a friend you have not spoken with for a while says, "I need help" in a dream, check out what is happening. If you dream about someone having surgery and afterward the doctor says, "It is fixed," you or the loved one will recover. Suppose you feel discouraged in your career and then dream that your boss shakes your hand, saying, "Congratulations on your promotion." You may want to work hard and persevere.

ADVANCED HINT # 4: DREAMS OFTEN SHOW LOGIC. Though a lot of dreams may appear disjointed, dreams can demonstrate a high amount of logic as they assess a problem or concern. When a dream has several scenes or parts, see if you can spot a sequential logic. For example, the first part may state the problem, the next might discuss what you have done about the concern or what has not worked, and the latter parts may recommend points to consider or directions that may resolve the issue.

ADVANCED HINT # 5: SENIORS OFTEN DREAM OF YOUNGER DAYS. Those fortunate enough to reach their eighties and nineties in good shape, often describe dreams that replay the days of their youth. These dreams often portray exact scenes of one's childhood or their earlier years, in great detail.

Sometimes these dreams of former years contain a message. At other times, they simply replay wondrous moments, cherished memories, or long-forgotten scenes of pain and trauma. As the years catch up, the waking mind dips into the past more often, and as we age, such retrospective thoughts are mirrored in our dreams.

Anecdotal reports by seniors suggest that dreams about their past are not distressing. Revisiting one's youthful memories often tends to comfort and uplift. Such dreams from one's early days may also be a way to prepare, ever so slowly, for a new, eternal adventure.

SERIAL DREAMING—
DREAMS THAT ARRIVE IN A SERIES

Noticing dreams that arrive *in a group* or *in a sequence* indicates that you have turned a corner in mastering dream analysis. Take a breath and have a look at the patterns you may meet in your dreams.

As if watching a television series, look for repetitive dreams that have similar stories or have repeating symbols. You can have a series of dreams about the same topic in a single night. Or, several dreams with the same story may occur over a period of days, weeks, or months. You may even notice symbols or backgrounds that keep cropping up. Take note. Every time a story line, symbol, or background element repeats in a dream, your psyche is working overtime to get your attention. It is up to you to find out why.

THE BOTTOM LINE ABOUT
ADVANCED DREAMING

Let your psyche lead the way to amazing dream insights when the time is right. Like a flower that unfolds or an oak tree that grows strong and tall, letting dream understanding proceed at a natural rate is always a good idea.

9

NIGHTMARES AND SCARY DREAMS: FRIGHTENING DREAMS ARE YOUR FRIEND

E VEN NIGHTMARES HAVE A HELPFUL PURPOSE. A nightmare is easy to recognize: You wake up feeling anything from mild fright to a complete terror that can leave you screaming. Yet even dreams that scare you come to help. The topic of a dream may well bring up a serious and intense message. However, the message comes from a friendly source—your own psyche—whose purpose is to help and support you. No matter how serious or scary the subject of the dream, the communication from your psyche is an attempt to help you resolve the matter or get through a challenging situation.

WHY A DREAM TURNS INTO A NIGHTMARE. Most nightmares are simply mirrors of your internal fears and anxieties. Paradoxically, as the following reasons explain, it is those very fears and anxieties that "flip" a dream that is otherwise benign into a nightmare.

Think of a dream as a carriage transporting a needed insight about an important problem; the carriage is merely a vehicle for the helpful message. However, the topic of the dream terrifies you. The topic could be about a failing relationship or a career that is falling apart. Because of your terror, as you watch the carriage approach, the shadows of your fears make the carriage look scary. You do not notice the carriage is driven by your psyche, who approaches as a friend and just wants to help.

One way of coping with an anxiety or fear is to distance yourself from it—to push it away. This is a normal reaction. Yet the very act of distancing yourself from a scary topic that a dream may address is what "transforms" a normal dream image into a scary one. It is like a tasty dish that curdles, and your fear curdles the dream dish.

THERE ARE ONLY FRIGHTENED DREAMERS. Though it is natural to run from what scares you, the very act of doing so is what often creates a nightmare. That is why one way of looking at most nightmares is to say, "There are no scary dreams—only frightened dreamers." If we could put aside all of our fears, there would be few nightmares or frightening dreams.

WHAT CAUSES NIGHTMARES. Mild to severe stress tends to be the main underlying cause of most frightening dreams.

- *Daily Stress.* Daily stress that ramps up your feelings is the most common reason behind a nightmare.

- *Out-of-Control Fear and Anxiety.* Like a wheel spinning out of control, negative emotions can unbalance your perceptions and lead to nightmares.

- *Emotional Dissonance.* The daily push-pull between competing feelings or choices is called "emotional dissonance." If making a choice feels so unpalatable and impossible that no choice seems right, the pressure can drive you to the edge. This form of extreme anxiety, related to difficult or impossible choices, often invites nightmares.

- *Physical or Mental Imbalance.* Conditions like fever or depression can produce bad dreams. When the condition passes, the nightmares may disappear.

- *Traumatic Events.* Repeated bad dreams can happen after a painful event that leaves you feeling vulnerable, such as losing a loved one or the loss of a home after a natural disaster. As the psyche tries to digest the pain, the mind may replay the event as a nightmare. Such dreams are the psyche's attempt to digest the painful feelings while you sleep. As a person heals and increases their coping skills, the bad dreams lessen and eventually disappear.

- *The Nightmares of Those with an Artistic or Sensitive Temperament.* Highly sensitive and creative individuals tune in more deeply to the world's pain and suffering, and as a result, they often report nightmares. A man at a seminar shared his constant nightmares about war scenes and mangled bodies, even though he lived a normal life and worked as a bus driver. Digging deeper, he began to see that he was tuning in to the daily pain that he saw on the faces of his passengers. Witnessing their distress gave his sensitive heart emotional indigestion, which he experienced as frequent nightmares.

- *Traumatic Stress.* Those with a medical condition called post-traumatic stress disorder, such as combat veterans or rape victims, can have nightmares that are different in content and structure to regular nightmares. Experiencing extreme forms of trauma can produce nightmares that are more severe and that disrupt sleep cycles, which regular nightmares do not. While researching the nightmares of combat veterans, I created presleep stories as a sleep aid that attempts to restore the normal sleep cycles of combat veterans; details are available at InterpretADream.com.

NIGHTMARES: THREE TYPES

Like other dreams, nightmares can be distinguished by their origin and purpose. The most common nightmares engage your struggle to grow in character and personality. A few bad dreams deal with specific life fears, and fewer still predict actual tragic events.

Type 1: The Most Common Type of Nightmare

A NIGHTMARE THAT UNVEILS A NEGATIVE CHARACTER TRAIT. Facing an unpleasant truth about yourself is never easy. Everyone glosses over shortcomings like anger, acting stupid, or failing at something, and no one wants to face a weakness. As a result, when a dream holds up a mirror about a trait that does not jive with your "I am great" image, your normal reaction is to say, "That can't be me." In colloquial terms, such nightmares expose your blind spots, which is an unpleasant experience for everyone.

For example, a man had a nightmare about a raging bull charging through his grocery store and wondered if the dream was a warning that vandals would soon raid his premises. Since most dreams are about you—the dreamer, he came to see that the bull was a metaphor for his short temper when dealing with employees. Seeing himself as an out-of-control bull was not easy, but the image produced the desired effect. The man softened his attitude and as a result, the atmosphere at the grocery store became more relaxed and as a bonus, his sales improved.

When a nightmare acts as a mirror of a not-so-great trait, it invites you to grow into a better version of yourself. After an initial "ouch," you realize that the dream is an ally, helping you correct what could cause problems down the road.

Type 2: A Scary Dream That You Meet Less Often

FRIGHTENING DREAMS THAT PORTRAY ACTUAL, SPECIFIC FEARS. One of the functions of dreaming is to process your emotions. When a fear gets out of hand, a nightmare that relates to that fear is the equivalent of a pressure cooker's safety valve that allows the hot steam to escape. In this case, the experience of having the nightmare, in and of itself, becomes an outlet for your exploding feelings.

Acting like an emotional digestion system, fear-processing nightmares let you experience a fear as an external picture that your mind can examine and label. A "see it, name it, and label it" nightmare helps you digest your fear, and as a result, whatever tied you up in knots begins to unravel. Such nightmares handle actual fears, one piece at a time, until they disappear. You may encounter a sequence of nightmares during a time of enormous challenge such as a divorce or the sudden loss of a loved one. Then one day, a morning arrives when you feel a sense of peace. You do not know why you feel better, but you know you have turned a corner. Your dream digestion system— that you experienced as nightmares—has done its work.

Nightmares that deal with true fears come with a bonus. A bad dream that relates to a painful issue can include an insight about how to handle what frightens you. A woman kept dreaming of a terrified young girl who walks to the edge of a murky black pond in the middle of the night. As she is about to fall into the deep black water, she sees a light in the distance and becomes aware that the light can lead her to safety. Upon discussion, those images brought back memories of the dreamer's terror of being raped as a young girl. The light in the distance made her realize that she could resolve the unexpressed pain that had been festering for years. Thanks to the dream's metaphor of a distant light as a place of safety, the dreamer became aware that she needed a counselor who could help her confront the emotional leftovers of her childhood trauma.

Type 3: Actual Warnings— A Rare Type of Frightening Dream

FRIGHTENING DREAMS AS TRUE WARNINGS. Most scary dreams are stress-related, a few may tussle with your actual fears, while a miniscule percent can be actual warnings about something dire. Nightmares can warn you about the possibility of a real tragedy that may involve death, serious illness, or a natural disaster—whether in your life, someone around you, or in your community. Or sometimes they are warnings about less serious matters.

LESS URGENT, YET TRUE WARNING DREAMS. Before examining frightening dreams that *are* dire warnings, let's take a look at dreams that address issues which are *not* life threatening, yet still urgent. For example, a dream may give you a heads up about how your words hurtfully impacted another's feelings that you missed, and as a painful issue, it becomes cloaked in scary images. Or, a dream may point out what will happen if you keep eating three desserts a day; seeing what you look like in a dream, with an extra fifty pounds on you, can be pretty scary. Or, a frightening dream may point out a topic such as an unpleasant relationship, that you have put on hold, which now needs attention. Because these less urgent issues deal with topics that make you anxious, the warning dream can still be experienced as a nightmare. Such not-so-dire warning dreams touch upon intense topics that are *not* life threatening, but can still intensely shake you up.

DREAM EXAMPLE: A FRIGHTENING DREAM ABOUT A NORMAL ISSUE— MY DAUGHTER IS IN A CAR CRASH. A mother dreamed that her daughter was in a car crash, and from a distance, she watched as her child was taken to the hospital. Afterward, a doctor announced that her daughter was okay. The dream felt so intense that the mother woke up terrified, fearing for her daughter's safety. The mother brought up her dream at a conference. A conversation brought out how, at the time of the dream, her only daughter announced that she was about to relocate because her new husband had been transferred to a job a thousand miles away. Since mom and daughter had never lived more than a few streets apart, the mother experienced a nightmare that registered her shock and distress at the news. Nothing terrible had happened. The nightmare simply registered the mother's reaction to the sudden, unexpected news of being separated from her daughter.

A TRUE WARNING NIGHTMARE ABOUT A POTENTIAL TRAGEDY. Though extremely rare, a nightmare can be a warning about an actual tragedy as a type of ESP dream, as in the following example.

DREAM EXAMPLE: A NIGHTMARE AS A TRUE WARNING—MY DAUGHTER IS IN A CAR CRASH. Another mother had several dreams that showed her only teenage daughter getting into a car with friends, then seeing the car in a deadly crash. Each time she had the dream, she debated whether to talk to her daughter about safe driving with her teenage friends but decided against it. Sadly, the repetitive dreams turned out to be an actual warning and she lost her only daughter. Meeting this woman at a seminar, I marveled at the grace with which the mother had resolved to learn about dreams, and to use future warnings for herself and loved ones. That took great courage.

Only the divine hand can know whether a tragedy foreshadowed in a dream can be averted. However, no matter how a predicted event turns out, such actual warning nightmares serve a constructive purpose. On the one hand, they give a dreamer time to build up their strength and cushion the shock of the actual event, if it comes about. On the other hand, according to stories exchanged in dream circles, such warning dreams can, at times, avert the real danger.

True dream warnings about dire events are extremely rare. They have noticeable features like repetition, intense emotions and literal details.

For more examples of nightmares and frightening dreams of every kind, have a look at the e-library of dreams at InterpretADream .com which is searchable by keyword.

10

PEOPLE IN DREAMS: WHEN ARE THEY MIRRORS OF YOU?

THE PEOPLE IN YOUR DREAMS. WHETHER THE person portrayed is a family member, friend, stranger, or someone rich and famous, each carries a unique message.

A DREAM CHARACTER AS A MIRROR: YOU SEE ONLY YOURSELF.

The most common purpose of a dream person is to mirror your own behavior and traits.

DREAM EXAMPLE: MY SISTER BEHAVED BADLY. A woman dreamed of her sister having a temper tantrum. In real life, her sister was capable of a grand explosion or two. The dreamer noted how insensitive her sister appeared in the dream as she spewed venomous words, and she suddenly remembered the verbal mudslinging that she, herself, had engaged in with a co-worker, the previous day. She realized that the dream scene described her, not her sister. Though normally professional and constructive, the previous day she lost her cool and her dream mirrored how she had appeared to coworkers. The dream made her realize that a kind word would have gone much further to resolve the situation than anger. When you see someone behaving badly in a dream, take a breath and fess up. In the end, most of the people that you dream about signify parts of yourself.

TO SEE WHETHER A PERSON IN A DREAM IS A MIRROR OF YOU, PLAY THE "TWO PLUS TWO" GAME

A DREAM PERSON AS A MIRROR OF YOU. "Projection" is a psychological term that describes how easy it is to see—in others—what you hide about yourself. Take the driver on the highway who weaves in and out of lanes, shouting at others about driving too slow or being in the wrong lane. He notices others' poor driving habits but is blind to his own. That is called projection. Instead of glaring at your own fault, you notice it in others.

Most people hate to admit to shortcomings like having a bad temper, eating or drinking too much, or not living up to their ideals. As you conveniently push away negative images of self in a dream, you let an actor "stand in" for you, to demonstrate the negative behavior that you hide from yourself. To further distance yourself from the flawed person that you don't want to recognize as really you—the stand-in takes on the appearance of a family member, a friend, or a stranger.

To explore how a dream person can mirror you, try this exercise. It is named the "Two Plus Two" game because you select two qualities and two shortcomings in a main dream character and then explore those traits in yourself. This is how it goes.

1. SELECT A DREAM PERSON.

- Select a prominent dream character who appeared in a recent dream. Choose someone who confused you or stimulated an intense reaction.

- Without thinking too much about it, list two positive traits and two negative traits about the dream person.

- Even if the dream character is a stranger or a well-known person who you do *not* know, you still have a notion of what they are like from their actions, appearance, and body language. Base your selections on those impressions and your reactions to the dream character.

- If the person is someone you know, list their actual traits that come to mind.

2. COULD THIS BE YOU? After listing the dream character's positive and negative traits, be bold. Examine the same traits in yourself. See which ones, if any, might apply to you at this time. Keep in mind that a trait may be relevant to you for only a limited time, or relate to you only in a specific situation. For example, you may normally be talkative, yet when troubled, you brood in silence. As a result, even though friends may describe you as chatty, a dream about a quiet person might portray you during a troubled phase.

3. BUT...WHAT IF THE PERSON IS NOT A MIRROR? After taking a good look, if you can sincerely conclude that the dream person's traits do not match yours, the character may not be a mirror of your traits or actions. Examine the alternative options about what dream characters may represent, as listed below.

DETERMINE WHEN A DREAM CHARACTER IS NOT A MIRROR OF YOU

Most of the time a dream person mirrors your personality and actions. However, there are exceptions. When a dream person does not fit as a mirror, explore these alternatives.

Alternative 1 of a Dream Person Who Is Not a Mirror

CHARACTERS MAY BE ACTING OUT A RELATIONSHIP DYNAMIC. Whether a dream relates to your relationship with a boss, an associate, family member, friend, or a love interest, people in dreams sometimes indicate how that relationship is going. Never ignore the story line; the story line is your first indication of who or what the dream is about. How characters behave in the dream *plus* the story line can unveil hidden motives, show how others see you, and reveal hidden agendas—yours and theirs.

When, in real life, you feel confused about a relationship, look for a dream that may mirror what is going on and shines a spotlight on the situation. A dream about a relationship can advise you how to handle others or invite you to tweak your own attitude or behavior.

Alternative 2 of a Dream Person Who Is Not a Mirror

A DREAM CHARACTER PORTRAYS AN ACTUAL PERSON. Once in a while a dream *is* truly about someone else. Such a dream may show the person acting and looking as they normally do. Or, it can be a metaphoric scene, but you recognize the topic and the qualities of the dream character as being related to someone else. A literal dream about another puts you in touch with their issues, reveals their talents, or gives insights about your role in their life. A woman who dreamed that a friend was contemplating suicide made a quick phone call. Thanks to the heads-up, the dreamer steered the friend back onto a positive track.

Alternative 3 of a Dream Person Who Is Not a Mirror

A DREAM CHARACTER GIVES DIRECT AND CLEAR GUIDANCE. A man or woman in a dream may at times directly present the information that you need, such as a family member pointing out where you misplaced a lost object or a mechanic working on a car part that needs to be replaced in your car. When that happens, no interpretation is necessary. Sometimes only the thought is implied, yet even if no words are spoken, the dreamer knows the intent. Whether words are spoken, thoughts implied, or a dream character demonstrates the information visually, the guidance can be direct and clear.

11

NOT ALL DREAMS ARE DREAMS: MYSTIC EXPERIENCES REMEMBERED AS DREAMS

NOT ALL DREAMS ARE DREAMS. BECAUSE A DREAM is a bridge between your nightly thoughts and your waking mind, author Stase Michaels suggests that a dream is your only vehicle of memory during sleep. If you have a mystical experience at night, you remember it as a dream because a dream is your only vehicle for memory at night. Though the argument of whether that is so is circular and speculative, anecdotal accounts are ripe with mystical dreams that are experienced as real events—often more real than can be captured by words. Mystical events remembered as dreams have their own signature and flavor, as explained in the following sections.

MYSTIC EVENTS HAPPEN MORE FREQUENTLY DURING SLEEP. Mystic and spiritual experiences tend to occur at night for several reasons. First, logic is placed on hold as you sleep, allowing the mind and soul to explore deeper depths and recesses of awareness. Second, there are no demands, no need for food or drink, and no enticements from electronic toys. As you drift into a peaceful sleep, your unfettered spirit is free to confer with the soul and explore what else is out there. Can anyone prove that mystical events take place during sleep? No, but dream enthusiasts regularly record fascinating examples, like the following.

DIVINE GRACES OFTEN HAPPEN DURING SLEEP. Some dreams are not dreams; they are experiences of divine grace. Whether you actively seek a blessing or it arrives as an unexpected gift, the divine hand at times sprinkles love, healing, and transformation as you sleep. As the New Testament bible phrase goes, "Seek and you will find, ask and you will receive." One way to recognize a dream that is a sprinkle of divine love is by the results. The dream brings a jolt of energy that leaves no doubt you have been touched by amazing grace. You feel a combination of shock, upliftment, joy, and transformation, though a precise description is beyond words, say those who have had this experience.

DREAM EXAMPLE 1 OF DIVINE GRACE IN A DREAM: CALL IF YOU NEED ME. A young woman drew on her deep faith as she struggled through a difficult job situation. Focusing on her work, she tried to keep a good attitude despite the constant bickering among her coworkers. However, by evening, she often collapsed into tears. One night she dreamed that she was flying through the air on a carpet. As a soft evening breeze flowed through her hair, the carpet landed on a mountaintop. A beam of light appeared from the sky, revealing a phone number in gold letters, one at time, with the numbers 777-7777. As each seven appeared, she was zapped with energy and joy. She felt as though her cup of love was overflowing, and then she woke with a start.

Recognizing seven as a mystical number in many traditions, she knew that God had smiled on her efforts to remain positive in a difficult situation. From that day forward, she sailed through her work days, shrugging off the discord. To her astonishment, within six months the troublemakers had left and were replaced by new associates who had kind and positive personalities. The unseen hand not only bestowed a healing grace on her, in a dream, but its effects also spilled over into her life, transforming a difficult workplace into a pleasant environment.

DREAM EXAMPLE 2 OF DIVINE GRACE IN A DREAM: JUST ASK. Over a one-year period, a man fervently sought to renew his spiritual path and experienced several dreams of amazing grace. These divine zaps encouraged yet shocked him, leading him to wonder if his night-time experiences were a fluke or could happen to anyone. One night, he prayed, "God, if someone seeks your favor, do you always respond? Are you really there?" That night a booming voice answered in a dream, "If you or anyone wants my help, you just need to ask." Like a strong wind that makes its presence felt, the message left him uplifted and joyous beyond words.

The Great Spirit had answered his question, leaving no doubt that God invites anyone to communicate and to ask for what they need. Such graces are often remembered as dreams. Some dreamers recount a direct physical healing; others speak of emotional healing in a dream as an answer to their prayers. Dreamers with these experiences describe feeling embraced by a divine love so strong that their lives are permanently altered. Most have a hard time finding words for their experience. However, all agree that there is an astonishing healing effect of the "love that surpasses all understanding" which they experienced, and say that it does not dim with time.

NIGHT MEETINGS WITH THOSE WHO HAVE PASSED ON. Loved ones who have died often appear in the dreams of family members and friends. The body of the deceased loved one often appears younger, whole, and full of life. Some say hello, others simply smile. Such nocturnal contacts hint that life is eternal. The encounters feel real and bring joy and consolation to the dreamer.

If your heart remains connected to a deceased loved one, they may say hello in a dream communication soon after passing or sometimes, years later. Such a visit by a deceased love one is remembered as a dream and may be a response to your feelings of loss. The person visits to assure you they are still alive in eternity, and in spirit. Such across-the-veil meetings are consistent with teachings about heaven and the afterlife that most religions mention but do not describe in detail.

Many believe the next realm of life is not far away in time or space, which allows loved ones who have passed on, to drop by. Mystics suggest that a bond of love makes it natural for a departed loved one to touch base from time to time, and bridging the gap between from afterlife to the dreamer is easiest during sleep.

Most dream visits by the dearly departed are marked by few words, though on occasion the deceased person may speak up. A striking example came from a father who died suddenly, about two years before his beloved daughter's wedding. A few weeks before her wedding day, the groom, who had never met her dad, told the bride's family about a dream that startled him. He described a dark-haired man with high cheek bones who said, firmly, three times, and each time louder than the last, "Take care of my daughter!" By the third time, the young man stammered, "Yes, sir," in response, in the dream.

The family laughed, recognizing the man in the groom's dream as the bride's father who had passed on. The dream brought back fond memories of how protective her dad had been toward his baby girl. Leaping across the veil, her dead father introduced himself to the groom. Though the husband-to-be was a fine young man, he reminded him that he wanted the best for his little girl. When there is love, family ties are eternal.

ASTRAL TRAVEL DURING DREAMS. Mystics claim that the soul can leave the body at night, during sleep, to take short jaunts. The experience is called "astral travel," also known as astral projection or an "out-of-body" experience. During astral travel, the sleeping body stays put while the soul soars out into the world and beyond, remaining connected to the body via a mystical thin, silver cord. The silver cord allows the soul to find its way back to its sleeping body.

TYPES OF ASTRAL TRAVEL. Anecdotal accounts report astral treks that give glimpses of other heavenly realms. Or, they can be journeys related to near-death experiences whereby a person dies or comes close to dying, visits the afterlife, but revives and lives to relate their experience. Astral travel can also happen during sleep—as a dream that is a mystic experience—remembered as a dream.

ASTRAL TRAVEL DREAMS. Some dreams of soaring down familiar streets at night, high above trees or buildings, may be experiences of astral travel. Ditto for dream scenes of enthusiastic chats with friends or associates that continue conversations that may have begun earlier in the day or renew a friendship, as a chat between friends. Astral travel dreams often depict real streets, people, and places that you recognize, and when you return from such night travels, the body may feel a jolt as it lands.

DREAM EXAMPLE 1 OF ASTRAL TRAVELS: A NIGHT VISIT WITH A FRIEND. A young woman who was concerned about a friend's health dreamed that she was flying through the air and hurtling over familiar city landmarks during the night. Fully aware of where she was, she soaked up the scene of glowing streetlights and deserted city roads. She arrived at her friend's home. Watching as the friend slept peacefully, she was assured that her friend was okay; the dreamer had accomplished her mission. She then realized that she had been away from home for a long time and was separated from her body. The awareness made her wake up with a jolt, as if her soul had landed back in to her body with a thud.

DREAM EXAMPLE 2 OF ASTRAL TRAVELS: A NIGHT STUDY SESSION.
Teachers with an interest in dreams report dream experiences of "night study sessions." Such dreams depict conversations with enthusiastic students that are a continuation of a topic that began in class, earlier in the day. The dreams feel real, like experiences of astral travel shared by a group, spurred to gather once again because of a mutual enthusiasm for a topic.

DREAM EXAMPLE 3 OF ASTRAL TRAVELS: JOURNEYS TO DISTANT LANDS. Dreamers report jaunts to distant lands to visit loved ones for a brief soul connection. Such an experience is common among twins separated by distance, or between married couples where one spouse is on deployment in a distant land. Details of conversations that take place during such a night visit may be forgotten, but the intense awareness of the connection they made with a loved one remains.

UNCHARTED TERRITORY. Such examples suggest that astral travel can be initiated by a concern for a loved one, a shared enthusiasm, or a longing for a loved one. Such heart links may initiate astral travels that are remembered as dreams. Mystics have described such experiences for centuries, which leave some to wonder how much we have yet to learn about uncharted soul horizons.

THE AUTHOR'S WISH FOR YOU

CONGRATULATIONS! YOU HAVE COMPLETED A trek through a few basic and several advanced notions about dreams and dreaming. The author hopes this brief glimpse into dreams leaves you ready, willing, and excited to explore your own life as retold to you in your dreams. Imparting a wish that you enjoy a lifetime of adventure by exploring your own dreams may sound a bit hackneyed—but it *is* my true wish for you.

THE AUTHOR'S PERSONAL WISH: TO SEE DREAMS TAUGHT IN SCHOOLS

My personal wish as a dream expert and enthusiast is to see dreams taught as a self-help tool in high school and college. In a world that is ever more challenging and that is accelerating technologically, empowering young people with self-help tools that promote constructive self-understanding and growth—such as dream analysis—would be a boon to one and all.

To further this daydream of seeing dreams taught in schools, I have put together an Introductory Course on Dream Analysis based on a lifetime of dream experience. *Newsflash*: This introductory course can work equally as an outline for teachers *and* as course content that a teacher can implement in his or her own style. I invite educators who are interested in teaching dream analysis, whether formally or informally, to contact me at InterpretADream.com, about this course.

Meantime, a fond farewell.

INDEX